MANX GIANT

FROM THE WONDERFUL ISLE OF MAN

The story of
Radio Caroline North
1964 - 1968

Andy Wint

Manx Giant from the Wonderful Isle of Man
Published by Chesterfield Publications
ISBN No. 978-0-9560139-0-3
Designed and Printed by The Copy Shop - 01624 622697

CONTENTS

Manx National Heritage is the statutory heritage agency for the Isle of Man and has a wide remit encompassing all aspects of our Island heritage. This includes museums, monuments, castles, art galleries, archives and scenic landscapes linked together through the "Story of Mann" portrayal throughout the Island. We cover everything from the activities of the Viking Norsemen, to the riders of Nortons in the TT motorbike races.

However, the story of this Island would not be complete without the story of the people themselves; their hopes and fears, their pastimes and their pleasures. Many museums and heritage organisations tend to forget this essential element of history. Not so for Manx National Heritage, which has, since the 1930's, collected the memories and impressions of Manx people and thereby preserved an otherwise undocumented element of our history for the future.

Sometimes, rarely, we come across an aspect of this previously undocumented history which provides a new insight into an historical event or a phenomenon which permeated a whole layer of society and made a lasting influence on all those who experienced it. Such was the importance for many of the "pirate" radio station, Radio Caroline North.

Although its story dates from only forty years ago, it illustrates how something from one generation's present can have such an influence that it becomes part of their heritage forever.

The story of Radio Caroline North, is inextricably linked with the Isle of Man. But it had a greater significance than its role in popular entertainment. The pioneering and innovative broadcasting model it created influenced the modern development of popular radio. It shaped the broadcasting landscape of the British Isles for over a generation and helped to define the modern constitutional relationship between the United Kingdom and the Isle of Man.

As far as we know, until Manx National Heritage developed its exhibition "Pirates of the Irish Sea" in 2008, no heritage organisation had seriously tackled this fascinating development in social history. We know from the many people who contacted us to contribute to the exhibition with their memories and exhibits, that Caroline is still fondly remembered in the hearts of many. No one remembers her more fondly than Andy Wint who has brilliantly documented in this book the spirit of those times, the ethos of Radio Caroline North, and its very special relationship with the Isle of Man. We have very much enjoyed working with Andy on this project and his book brings back very happy memories for all of us who succumbed to Caroline's illicit charms across the airwaves of our youth.

Stephen Harrison
Director - Manx National Heritage
July 2008

CHAPTER 1

RONAN O'RAHILLY

"If after managing my own artists I have to create my own record label because nobody will record them and if I then find that no radio station will play their music, it seems that the only thing now is to have my own radio station."

Ronan O'Rahilly at a meeting with Radio Luxembourg

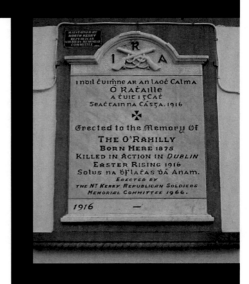

RONAN O'RAHILLY

Born in 1939 the son of Aodogán and Marion O'Rahilly. Ronan was the grandson of Michael O'Rahilly, an Irish nationalist who was shot and killed during the Easter Rising in 1916. Aodogán (1904-2000) was a highly educated and successful businessman with extensive interests in manufacturing and shipping, Marion (1905-1994 nee O'Connor) was born in America. They married in 1934 and lived in a large house in the leafy Dublin suburb of Clondalkin where Ronan and siblings Nuala, Eoin, Roisín and Iseult were raised.

Aodogán O'Rahilly would have been aware of the power of radio. Irish nationalists had broadcast news of the Easter Rising via Morse code using a ship's transmitter housed at the School of Wireless Telegraphy in O'Connell Street, Dublin. Rigid censorship by the British had previously prevented details of the conflict reaching the outside world but these makeshift radio broadcasts made it front page news. Aodogán moved in government and business circles at the highest level, he was a member of the Turf Development Board (peat was an extremely important state asset especially during World War II when lack of shipping meant Ireland had to produce its own energy), manufactured roof tiles, started one of the biggest private forestry plantations in Ireland specialising in 'Leprechaun' Christmas trees and significantly bought Greenore Port in County Louth in 1959 forming Greenore Ferry Services Ltd.

Ronan gravitated to London in 1961 where he ran a nightclub and managed pop musicians and singers including Georgie Fame. He financed an independent recording of a Georgie Fame track and succeeded in getting it released. Publicity via airplay was another matter. The BBC Light Programme didn't play new artists and the only other outlet, Radio Luxembourg, leased their programmes to the big record labels EMI, Decca, Pye and Philips. New talent seemingly had no place to go. Ronan then heard about radio stations on ships broadcasting to Scandinavia and Holland. He was approached by the Radio Atlanta consortium with a view to joining their project. All that was needed was financial backing and an out-of-the-way port to convert the ship.

OUTLAWS *May* USE SUPER-STATIONS *at Sea*

by MURPHY McHENRY

RADIO circles on the Pacific Coast were turned topsy turvy not long ago by the continued presence of a radio pirate ship which had taken unto itself a very popular spot on the dial and started broadcasting without regard for the land stations with which it interfered.

The primary purpose of the unlicensed broadcast station was to advertise the gambling, liquor, and other dubious pleasure activities of the ship upon which it was built—all these activities beyond the 12-mile limit, of course. Thousands responded to the advertising and the owners waxed rich. They found other sundry rackets, such as a fortune telling program, which brought in additional money and finally assumed such an extensive program that one Los Angeles station was threatened with a complete loss of audience and business because the ship's radio signal was the more powerful of the two.

After numerous unsuccessful attempts of a local nature, the floating broadcasting establishment was silenced, but only after the state department at Washington, D. C., had made diplomatic representations which forced a Central

U. S. Radio inspectors are here shown as they check on outlaw stations, gathering evidence to prove that their waves are carried beyond state boundaries.

Map showing locations of several stations just across border in Mexico. Gulf of Mexico, to which several stations may be driven, is also pictured. XEPN's balloon aerial blew away.

This is one of the several super-sensitive directional antennas used by officials of the federal radio commission to keep a constant check on the hundreds of radio stations in the U. S.

Broadcasting stations without a country seek new ways to flood the United States with radio advertising barred by federal commission. Two hundred outlaws face war by the government.

American country to cancel the ship's registry.

However, this ship had paved the way and now, with the United States making headway in its fight to muzzle stations just south of the Rio Grande river, within the shelter of Mexico, it appears that soon floating broadcast palaces may be dotted here and there outside the 12 mile limit, particularly in the Gulf of Mexico.

There is little chance that the border broadcasters will give up without a struggle. Led by XER's spectacular Dr. John R. Brinkley, formerly of Milford, Kansas, and now of Del Rio, Texas, they have found too many ways to gather in otherwise hard earned dollars to sit by complacently and be permanently hushed. Dr. Brinkley has made millions of dollars as a result of his broadcasts. Others, working along numerous lines, have taken in many more millions.

And that is why, in the face of possibilities that they may be driven out of Mexico, these promotional minded broadcasters

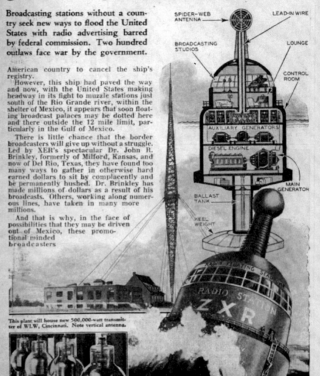

SPIDER—WEB ANTENNA — LEAD-IN WIRE
BROADCASTING STUDIOS — LOUNGE
CONTROL ROOM
AUXILIARY GENERATORS
DIESEL ENGINE
MAIN GENERATOR
BALLAST TANK
KEEL WEIGHT
RADIO STATION ZXR

This plant will house new 500,000-watt transmitter of WLW, Cincinnati. Note vertical antenna.

Here is the artist's conception of how the broadcasting stations now proposed for sea use may look. Water forms a perfect ground for broadcasting purposes and it is freely predicted that outlaw stations, those denied the privilege of broadcasting on United States soil, would attain even greater coverage if they had proper equipment anchored outside the 12-mile zone on the Gulf of Mexico. Below, left, are seen several of the huge new tubes which will be used in feeding 500,000 watts power into WLW's antenna. Outlaws are already planning to compete with this huge output.

Border Blaster Cities

1 Tijuana	6. Piedras Negras
2 Rosarito	7 Monterray
3 Nogales	8 Neuvo Laredo
4 Cd Juarez	9 Matamoros
5 Cd Avuña	10 Tampico

UNITED STATES

MEXICO

CHAPTER 2

John Brinkley

Wolfman Jack

Cross Border Radio exists when a licensed radio station deliberately transmits at very high power from a location in one country to listeners in a separate country. The first examples of this phenomenon arrived in the US in the 1920s when renegade broadcasters such as John Brinkley sought to broadcast to America from Mexico. From the 1920s to the '70s, using broadcasting signals far in excess of US stations, the Mexican 'Border Blasters' could be heard across a large swathe of the US, to the great irritation of American radio stations. Additionally, whereas American stations begin with the call letters K or W and Canadian stations with C the Mexican radio station has an air of mystery which adds to their allure; their call sign prefix is X, itself a symbol of ambiguity and inscrutability. All perfect fodder for the 1972 George Lucas film American Graffiti which featured the howling dj Wolfman Jack broadcasting from 'XERB in Mexico' to amorous teenagers in early 1960s Southern California; it seems even Hollywood directors listened to Cross Border Radio.

11

CROSS BORDER RADIO

John Brinkley (1885-1942) was a contentious American medical doctor who experimented with transplants of animal testicular glands into humans as a means of restoring male impotence. In the world of radio he broke new ground by establishing the age of Cross Border Radio.

A quack doctor whose trick was to insert goats' testicles into humans, Brinkley had a knack for publicity. He used newspapers, direct mail, then, in 1923, his own radio station KFKB in Kansas. In between live performances by singers and musicians he would promote his medical treatments available at 'affiliated' pharmacies only. The American Medical Association and Federal Radio Commission disapproved and in 1930 both his medical and radio license were revoked. After unsuccessfully attempting to regain both his Kansas medical and radio

license he relocated to Del Rio, Texas. While there he hit upon the idea of broadcasting from Mexico to the US. In 1931 he got a Mexican government license for a 75 kW station on 840 kHz AM. His station, at Villa Acuña was located on the opposite side of the Rio Grande from Del Rio, he simply rented a landline from his studio in Texas to the transmitter in Mexico.

Under the call sign of XER Brinkley used his new station to resume his medical practice and run a political campaign for Governor. The station could be heard as far north as Canada. Whilst his political ambitions remained frustrated his coffers overflowed. Male listeners were offered an array of expensive concoctions which included Mercurochrome injections and pills, all designed to help them regain their sexual prowess. At his clinic he also performed prostate operations. It is reported that he performed over 16,000 operations, at $600 ($7,000 today) a time, to combat male impotence. It has been claimed that up to 1938 Brinkley earned $12 million.

Other American promoters became inspired by the advent of Cross Border Radio and

many new stations were added along various points of the borders of Mexico with the United States.

Brinkley's days were numbered though, with the advent of World War II he extended his support to the sympathisers of Nazi Germany by allowing them airtime. Although before the bombing of Pearl Harbour and the US declaration of war it was a step too far for the US government. In April 1941, the Mexican Government made a deal with the United States to restrict renegade stations such as XERA putting Brinkley's station out of business. The United States banned cross-border links between US radio studios and Mexican transmitters without a US license with legislation which became known as the Brinkley Act.

'Doctor' Brinkley's final years were not distinguished; he had lost his radio station; several of his former patients sued him for malpractice; the Internal Revenue Service indicted him for tax evasion and the US Postal Service for mail fraud. He was declared bankrupt in 1941. He then suffered three heart attacks and lost a leg to poor circulation. He died impoverished in San Antonio.

CROSS BORDER RADIO

Britain has its own Cross Border Radio chronicle concerning a man called Captain Plugge. Leonard Plugge (1889-1981) was a businessman, Tory MP for Chatham and broadcasting pioneer. Plugge was also a fan of motoring holidays on the continent. During one holiday he stopped in the Normandy coastal village of Fécamp. In conversation he discovered that a member of the Le Grand family, which owned the town's Benedictine distillery, had a radio transmitter which was used periodically. Plugge offered to buy airtime to broadcast programmes in English to England from Normandy and Radio Normandy was born. A makeshift studio was fashioned from which the programmes were broadcast by Plugge's announcers, including Max Stanniforth, Stephen Williams, Bob Danvers-Walker and David Davies. Davies later became Managing Director of the South Africa-bound Cross Border Mozambique broadcaster Lourenco Marques Radio.

Not content with just one station Plugge created the International Broadcasting Company in 1931 as a commercial rival to the BBC by renting airtime from radio stations such as Normandy, Toulouse, Juan les Pins,

Poste Parisien, Barcelona and Rome and selling sponsorship to British companies who wanted to reach listeners to the new phenomenon of 'wireless'. IBC also sold advertising for Radio Luxembourg until 1936.

Radio Normandy's transmitter power was increased after Plugge came to an agreement with Gaumont British, the film studio proprietors, owner of 280 picture houses and, importantly, publishers of the entertainment-based Sunday newspaper Sunday Referee. Hitherto the press and BBC had been openly hostile but now Plugge had an ally; someone who would print his programme schedule. A new studio was established and Radio Normandy's large audience, extending as far north as the English Midlands was getting bigger. Colonel Richard L. Meyer was appointed General Manager of IBC and top entertainment stars of the day were featured on shows recorded in IBC studios and on location at theatres. The recordings, on movie film soundtrack and large recording discs, were played back in Normandy and the listening public back home lapped up the entertainment which contrasted sharply to John Reith's BBC output, especially on Sundays. Under Reith

the BBC wasn't on-air until late on Sundays to give people time to go to church. Things were set fair but, unfortunately for Plugge, fate intervened and World War II began, Radio Normandy went off the air and on 10 June 1940 French troops sabotaged the transmitter on the eve of the German invasion.

During World War II Cross Border Radio took on a more furtive guise with all combatants engaging in 'Black Propaganda'. On the Axis side it ranged from the faintly absurd 'Germany Calling' Nazi broadcasts to the UK and US by the adenoidal William Joyce and others as 'Lord Haw-Haw' on the Reichssender Hamburg; 'Tokyo Rose', who delivered propaganda in the South Pacific from Radio Tokyo and was mostly identified as Iva Toguri D'Aquino but played also by Ruth Hayakawa, June 'The Nightingale of Nanking'Suyama and Myrtle 'Little Margie' Lipton who additionally broadcast from

CROSS BORDER RADIO

Japanese-controlled Radio Manila and 'Axis Sally' aka Mildred Gillars whose anti-semitic rhetoric was broadcast from Radio Berlin to Allied troops, often speculating on the faithfulness of their wives and sweethearts.

Soldatensender Calais was one of the British responses. It was operated from 1943 to 1945 by the Political Warfare Executive and was, ostensibly, a station of the German military broadcasting network called 'Soldier's Radio Calais' *Soldatensender Calais* operated from 6pm to dawn and unlike its predecessor *Gustav Siegfried Eins* was broadcast live from the purpose-built broadcast studio at Milton Bryan, on the edge of the Woburn Abbey Estate in Bedforshire by announcers including the actor Marius Goring who spoke impeccable German. It operated on Medium Wave 833 kHz (360m), 714 kHz (420 m), and 612 kHz (490 m) with an associated shortwave station. It used 'Aspidistra' a 600-kilowatt RCA transmitter built for radio station WLW of Cincinnati but rendered unusable after the Federal Communications Commission imposed a 50 kw power limit. 'Aspidistra' was, at the time, the world's largest medium wave transmitter and was housed in an underground bunker in Crowborough, Sussex. The station used a mixture of music, relays of speeches by Hitler and others, coverage of sport and current events interlaced with morale decreasing items such as warnings of confidence tricksters swindling German soldiers into being transferred from France to the Russian front. During the D-Day invasion of June 6, 1944, *Soldatensender Calais* broadcast information that the invasion area was much wider than it actually was. After the Pas de Calais area was overrun, the station changed its callsign to *Soldatensender West* and closed down without ceremony soon after.

After hostilities ceased Captain Plugge hoped to go back to the old days and restart transmissions from France but changes in broadcasting regulations and a different attitude to radio listening meant it would never happen. After the war, IBC became a successful recording studio instead and many famous stars including The Rolling Stones, The Kinks, The Who and Jimi Hendrix graced its portals.

If the BBC thought that with Plugge out of the way it could relax - it was misguided; an identical situation had developed featuring Radio Luxembourg. But it wasn't just Britain which was faced with Cross Border Radio. France had been bombarded with 'Radios Périphériques' since the 1930s with Radio Luxembourg from Luxembourg, Radio Andorre and Sud Radio from Andorra, Radio Monte Carlo from Monaco, and Europe 1 from Saarland, Germany all broadcasting legally across international borders at one time or another. This situation persisted, much to the annoyance of radio entrepreneurs in France, until the legalisation of private broadcasting within La Republique in the early 1980s.

The British government disdainfully identified stations like Radio Luxembourg as pirates because their intended audience was in the United Kingdom. The broadcasts were considered illegal on British soil as these stations were breaking the monopoly of the non-commercial BBC.

Unbelievably, listening to the broadcasts was technically a violation of UK radio-licence laws.

Additionally, even though contemporary technology would have easily permitted it, Radio Luxembourg wasn't allowed to broadcast live from its West End studios in Hertford Street as the GPO telephone monopoly forbade the linking of studios to Luxembourg's transmitters.

Often referred to as the Radio Luxembourg of South Africa LM Radio (Lourenço Marques Radio) was a privately owned and operated radio station broadcasting to Southern Africa from Lourenço Marques (now Maputo), Mozambique between 1933 and 1975.

Radio in Lourenço Marques began in 1933. From 1935 Radio Clube de Moçambique was launched, broadcasting mostly in English. In 1947, John Davenport and Colonel Richard L. Meyer, previously General Manager of the International Broadcasting Company formed Davenport & Meyer to take over the running of Lourenço Marques Radio. They recruited David Davies, also formerly of IBC to run the station. In 1948

LM Radio moved into the 'Radio Palace', a purpose built 4-storey building and started producing variety shows in front of live audiences. Things were looking up. From its inception radio broadcasting in South Africa had been provided by the state owned and operated SABC (South African Broadcasting Corporation) with unsurprising consequences. The late 1950s brought the immense worldwide appetite from youngsters for rock'n'roll and pop music and the response came from LM Radio. The station underwent a major format change to cater for younger listeners who were ignored in South Africa by SABC. LM Radio introduced its renowned LM Hit Parade and played a major part in promoting South African artists and music. Many a South African artist made their professional debut on LM Radio at the frequent road shows which freely toured South Africa and much South African announcing talent including John Berks, Gary Edwards, Frank Sanders, John Grierson, Robin Alexander, George Wayne and David Gresham all started at LM Radio before moving to other positions. In 1969 Meyer left LM Radio and much of its sparkle went; it was taken over by the SABC in 1972.

CROSS BORDER RADIO

Politics arrived on September 7 1974 when the station was occupied during a bloody uprising the administration of the station was taken over by the Frelimo army. In October 1975, following Mozambican independence from Portugal, LM Radio facilities were nationalised and the station closed down. In South Africa SABC Radio 5 took its place, staffed by many former LM announcers.

Colonel Richard L. Meyer

I taught them everything they know, but not everything I know.

James Brown

CHAPTER 3

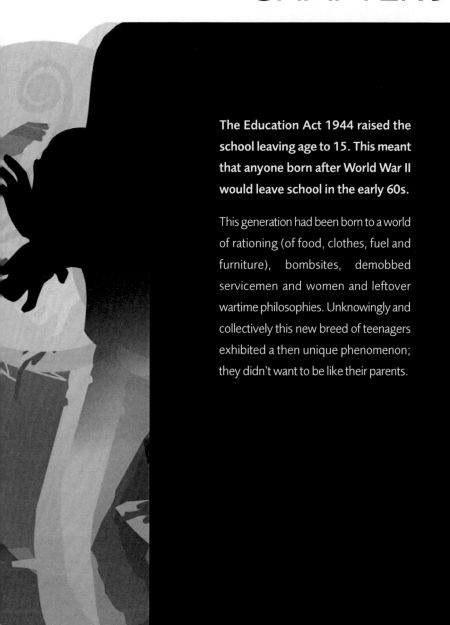

The Education Act 1944 raised the school leaving age to 15. This meant that anyone born after World War II would leave school in the early 60s.

This generation had been born to a world of rationing (of food, clothes, fuel and furniture), bombsites, demobbed servicemen and women and leftover wartime philosophies. Unknowingly and collectively this new breed of teenagers exhibited a then unique phenomenon; they didn't want to be like their parents.

EARLY 60'S BLUES

They were aspirational and better educated than any equivalent generation before. There was full employment, hire purchase and the contraceptive pill. Life, they had decided, was for living; especially with the newly-created ever present threat of nuclear annihilation as a backdrop. They embraced life and their own distinct culture; they didn't dress like their parents, didn't act like their parents and didn't enjoy the same music. They knew what they liked and bought the records by the millions.

For their immediate elders, born during the ten years previous and not having been active combatants, the post-war grammar schools, art colleges and embryonic comprehensive schools had provided the stepladder to higher and further education, better jobs and elevated ambitions. Hundreds of thousands of working class kids who would previously have headed for manual labour and apprenticeships formed the working class seed corn which was planted in all sectors of society and every industry; including the pop music industry.

The explosion of rock'n'roll in the mid-fifties had fizzled out. Elvis was in the US Army, Little Richard had turned to religion, Chuck Berry was in jail, Buddy Holly dead and Jerry Lee Lewis disgraced. The old guard of show business ran things in Britain just as in America. Demarcation lines were fixed with each protagonist knowing his or her place in the order of things. Whether writer, publisher, record label, manager, agent, booker, producer, arranger or artist; each knew what their situation was. But the catalyst was on the way; the generation which spawned a new strain of photographers, cinema directors and actors, TV directors, fashion designers and models, authors and playwrights was heading for the pop business.

In Liverpool, Manchester, London, Belfast, Birmingham, Newcastle and all points in between young men were absorbing influences and stating their musical credentials in the thousands of pop groups which sprang from youth clubs, coffee bars and church halls. Those who made it required management and administration and it was here that the alternative lay. Instead of hiring the established confederation of entertainment professionals an innovative option appeared; they, or their kind, would

EARLY 60'S BLUES

do it themselves. Thus artists began to write their own songs and music, produce and own their own recordings, have a manager who understood and fought for them, even own their own record label.

Thus it was in 1963 when a highly talented keyboard player and singer from Leigh, Lancashire called Clive Powell gained a manager called Ronan O'Rahilly; a creative young Irishman active in the West London beat scene. Clive, with typical 60s self-confidence, became Georgie Fame and Ronan, unable to get a recording deal financed a studio session which resulted in a track called 'Let The Sun Shine In'. He convinced a smaller label (CBS) to release it but had no luck in getting radio airplay; the BBC haughtily dismissed the very notion of a new artist, Radio Luxembourg pointed out the commercial realities of their operation to him. But that wasn't the end of that. A group of enterprising Scandinavians, Texans and Dutchmen had blazed a trail which O'Rahilly learned of.

199 CAROLINE

The MV Fredericia during fitting out in Fredikshavn

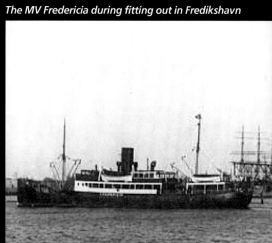

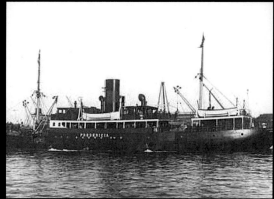

CHAPTER 4

Offshore radio refers to the broadcasting of radio signals from ships or fixed maritime structures outside the jurisdiction of a sovereign state.

But is it Offshore Radio or Pirate Radio? The 1950s Danish press can take the blame for the 'Pirate Radio' tag as they began to use the expression 'Pirate Radio' about Radio Mercur. A number of cartoons in newspapers and magazines pictured the radio station with pirate symbols. Thus an image was created. But it was Gordon McLendon, the American radio genius who was a major catalyst in developing European offshore radio.

By the time Radio Caroline North anchored in Ramsey Bay in July 1964 offshore radio was well-established.

Radio Mercur offices

The majority of offshore broadcasters have, however, been unlicensed radio stations using seaborne broadcasting as a means to circumvent national broadcasting regulations primarily for financial gain. Nonetheless, the practice has been used by state broadcasting organisations (such as The Voice of America) as a means of thwarting the broadcasting regulations of other nations. Indeed the UK Labour government was said to be planning an offshore radio station on board HMS Leviathan off the coast of Mozambique in 1966 to broadcast propaganda to Ian Smith's post UDI Rhodesia. Perhaps UK Prime Minister Harold Wilson, listening in his Huyton constituency, got inspiration from Caroline North?

In 1952 the Voice of America installed a studio and relay facility on *USCGC Courier*. The targets of her 150kw transmitter were the hearts and minds of listeners in Russia and her Iron Curtain allies. The *Courier* was originally intended to become the first in a fleet of mobile, radio broadcasting ships that built on the US Navy's experience during World War II in using warships as floating broadcasting stations. The *Courier* eventually dropped anchor off Rhodes in the Mediterranean with the complicit approval of the Greek government. This VOA relay station stayed on the air until the 1964 when facilities were eventually provided on land. Unknowingly the *Courier* and the US government supplied training to engineers who later worked on several of the European commercial offshore broadcasting stations of the 1950s and 1960s

The claim to be the first commercial offshore radio station in the world and thus to have inspired the rest sits with Radio Mercur, a Danish station which started 2 August 1958 and ceased officially on 31 July 1962. She broadcast from *MV Cheeta* anchored between Copenhagen and Malmo. Mercur's owners' contention was that radio transmissions from an anchored ship in international waters were not regulated by domestic legislation. Thus this hybrid of the cross-border Radio Luxembourg and the Voice of America relay on board the *USCGC Courier* became the inspiration for offshore radio. The accomplishment of Radio Mercur proved unequivocal motivation for three groups of enthusiastic businessmen to start their own ventures in Sweden and Holland.

THE IDEA

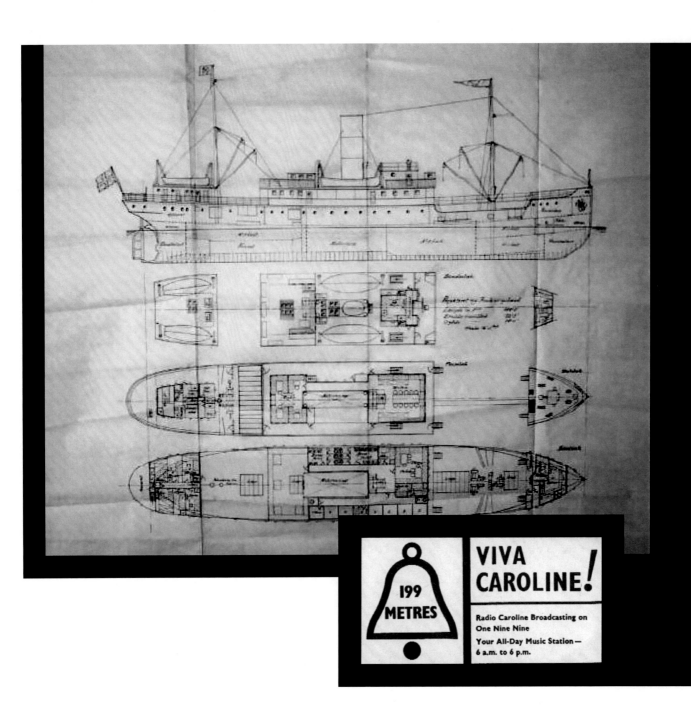

In December 1958 Skånes Radio Mercur was the first offshore station to broadcast to Sweden albeit from the Danish ship Radio Mercur. Nils-Eric Svensson leased air time from Radio Mercur to broadcast pop music to the densely populated south western tip of Sweden. Swedish state radio played hardly any pop music so the broadcasts were a big success. Svensson's operation lasted for three years until he sold the station in 1961 to one of the station's marketing executives Britt Wadner. She not only bought the station but purchased the transmission vessel MV Cheeta Mercur from Radio Mercur to create Radio Syd. Thus, in 1961 Sweden found itself with two offshore stations; Radio Nord (North) situated in the Stockolm archipelago and Radio Syd (South) off Malmo. Britt Wadner, an ex-beauty queen, went in and out of jail as a celebrity criminal when Radio Syd continued to defy Swedish legislation and in 1964 she bought a larger vessel, MV Cheeta II from the former Radio Mercur. Radio Syd finally ceased transmissions to Sweden in 1966.

Radio Nord was the Swedish station which operated from 8 March 1961 to 30 June 1962 from the MS Bon Jour anchored off Stockholm. Again, christened 'pirate' Radio Nord operated within the laws of the day and its offices were located in the heart of Stockholm. Tellingly, its ownership was vested in a company which had been specifically formed by Texan broadcasting and political interests.

In June 1960 the hold of the MS Olga had been converted in Hamburg into studios, transmitter room and crew quarters. Due to laws restricting the unlicensed installation of broadcasting equipment at the port, the ship, now renamed MS Bon Jour, was taken to Langeline the Freeport in Copenhagen. A 42 metre antenna mast was erected and two 10 kilowatt Continental Electronics transmitters, supplied from Dallas in six thousand pieces, had been assembled and installed.

The Swedish government flexed it muscles and empowered the authorities to seize Radio Nord's technical equipment if she ever entered a Swedish port and put diplomatic pressure on her country of registration (Nicaragua) to withdraw the certificate. The owners of the ship promptly renamed the vessel MV Magda Maria and registered her in Panama. Radio Nord's mixture of music,

about
RADIO CAROLINE

RADIO CAROLINE 199m.

RADIO CAROLINE 199 METRES

CAROLINE

features and magazine programming was fashionable and extremely popular but, following the passing of restrictive legislation, Radio Nord ceased broadcasting at the end of June 1962. For the ship this was just the end of one offshore chapter as on July 4, the *MV Magda Maria* was bound for El Ferrol in Spain. She docked on August 2 1962 and after certain repairs were carried out under the new name of *MV Mi Amigo* a new phase in her eventful life would await.

On October 15 1959 at the Krasnapolsky Hotel in Amsterdam a consortium called VRON (Vrije Radio Omroep Nederland - Free Radio Station of the Netherlands) was set up by a group of radio, TV and white goods retailers. They sought to advance the sales of their radio receivers by broadcasting more popular programmes than the establishment, state-licensed stations. Radio Veronica began broadcasting pop music from a former lightship *Borkum Riff* on 21 April 1960. It became the most popular station in the Netherlands and for a short time ran an English service called CNBC (Commercial Neutral Broadcasting Company). Programmes were recorded in a studio in Hilversum and played out on the ship by engineers, live

news broadcasts were read by announcers on board. By the end of the 1960s the studios and offices moved to bigger premises and a newer vessel the *MV Norderney* was used until Radio Veronica closed down on August 31 1974 to start the, ultimately successful, campaign for land-based status.

Gordon McLendon (1921-1986) was one of America's radio greats as a broadcaster, innovator and entrepreneur. A 1994 inductee of the Radio Hall of Fame McLendon is credited for perfecting the Top 40 format, pioneering sports and all-news broadcasting and originating the 'Beautiful Music' format. He attended Yale University, fought in World War II and whilst on course for a Harvard Law qualification left to enter the world of radio. He founded the phenomenally successful KLIF Radio in Dallas and the Liberty Radio Network, famous for its daily broadcasts of live and re-created Major League Baseball games. After entering the primary for the 1968 Texas gubernatorial election he departed from both the election and the Democratic Party, citing President Johnson's Vietnam War policies. Clint Murchison (1923-1987) was the founder of the Dallas Cowboys NFL team; he had

THE IDEA

business links to the oil industry, construction, real estate and European offshore radio. Murchison and his colleague Robert Thompson backed Gordon McLendon and Scandinavian businessman Jack Kotschack to create Radio Nord. Both from Texas, Murchison and McLendon as young boys would have heard the 1930s border-blasters from Mexico.

CHAPTER 5

GREENORE

Greenore Port located on the southern shore of Carlingford Lough was the Irish sea terminal for the Dundalk, Newry and Greenore Railway which dated back to 1873. The London North Western Railway's ambitions to secure a slice of the Irish Sea traffic to connect with its Euston to Holyhead service led it to invest in Greenore as the link in this lucrative connection. Greenore village was built to provide accommodation for the port and railway workers. The LNWR built a lavish hotel to serve passengers using the ferry to Heysham, Fleetwood and Holyhead.

Upon amalgamation of UK railway companies the DNGR passed to the London Midland & Scottish Railway in 1923 however partition of Ireland in 1921 had deemed that the DNGR now straddled the Northern Ireland/Irish Free State border thus affecting long-established patterns of commerce between formerly friendly neighbours. Previously cursory Customs examinations became protracted affairs delaying consignment of goods and affecting livestock shipments particularly. Passenger steamers stopped in 1926. Losses increased and in 1933 The Great Northern Railway (Ireland) took the reins but the end was not far away.

The British Transport Commission took ownership in 1948 and decided not to continue the subsidy which had been keeping the line operational; it was closed at the end of 1951 although the tortuous winding up procedure and sale of assets was only finally concluded in July 1954.

Aodogàn O'Rahilly, Ronan's father, purchased Greenore Port with a view to establishing Ireland's foremost container port. It was from here that he exported his brand of Christmas trees to England. But it was in March 1964 that this sleepy, seldom used port became the hub of the offshore radio world; O'Rahilly senior permitted it to become the centre of operations for fitting-out both Radio Caroline and Radio Atlanta.

The MV Fredericia arrived at Greenore on March 5 1964 for conversion to a radio ship. The 165 foot mast was erected by the Greenore crane crew; 30 tons of concrete ballast added to counterbalance the antenna, a large anchor system installed, studios installed, the ship renamed MV Caroline and registered in Panama. Three weeks later the work completed she departed March 26 with Captain Baeker giving her destination as

GREENORE

Spain. In fact she made for the Thames Estuary and anchored off Felixstowe; her inaugural broadcast being made on Easter Saturday March 28. The Radio Atlanta ship MV Mi Amigo arrived shortly after the MV Caroline and departed two days after her but was delayed in reaching the Thames Estuary finally commencing broadcasts on April 27.

The O'Rahilly family sold their interest in Greenore in 2002. The Port continues its activities today with a €27m development in the offing which may see the return of ferries.

MV Caroline and MV Mi Amigo at Greenore

Alan Turner

Captain Baeker

Generating the power courtesy of Daimler Benz

34

CHAPTER 6

MV Caroline

Originally *MV Fredericia* a Danish passenger ferry for the DFDS line

Tonnage: 763

Built: 1930 V & F A/S in Frederikshavn Denmark

Length: 118 feet

Beam: 32' 3"

Power: 100hp diesel engine single screw

Speed: Capable of 14 knots

36

The first commercial (promoting Woburn Abbey) on Radio Caroline was broadcast on May 1 1964. More customers keen to reach the growing audience followed; but there was a stumbling block. The leading advertising agencies were wary of this new industry for two reasons; firstly the unknown territory of daytime commercial radio led to a circumspect attitude towards clients' funds and secondly there were scare stories about the legality of the operation spread by rival operators in allied fields. Revenue was in the doldrums and with initial capital running out fiscal necessity led Planet Productions (Caroline) and Project Atlanta together and saw them return to the original agreement of *MV Caroline* covering the north and *MV Mi Amigo* covering the south. There would be a difference though; Atlanta would disappear from the air and the Caroline name would prevail. Ronan O'Rahilly had won an important skirmish. On Thursday July 2, the merger was formally announced to the City.

The on-air mechanic was splendidly simple; Radio Atlanta on board *MV Mi Amigo* would close down in the evening and simply reopen next day as Radio Caroline South, the original Radio Caroline close down and *MV Caroline* would sail to her new home and become Radio Caroline North.

The decision about how to publicise the, ostensibly, new radio station arose; certainly the industry would find out through the usual channels but what about the millions of listeners? Unsurprisingly the flamboyant O'Rahilly had an idea which created a virtue out of necessity. Instead of simply closing down at the East Anglian anchorage and opening up when they got to their destination in the north, which would have been functional and sufficient, he wanted to shout from the rooftops. The decision was taken to broadcast continuously as the ship sailed, creating news and publicity as she went. On Friday July 3 1964 *MV Caroline* weighed anchor and departed the Thames Estuary under the command of Captain Abraham Hengefeld.

The voyage was a bravura coup of public relations and guaranteed an avalanche of coverage across the weekend. The resort towns and villages along the Kent, Sussex, Hampshire, Dorset, Devon, Cornish and Welsh coasts were buzzing with the news as the ship with the tall mast sailed by.

HARWICH TO RAMSEY

Listeners inland followed the broadcast minute by minute, their imaginations fired by the audacity and panache of the concept. Newspapers and television feasted upon the images of Tom Lodge, Alan Turner and Jerry Leighton broadcasting live as they sailed around the coast; there had been nothing like it before in the history of British broadcasting. The Caroline North story had begun.

Essex Girl - PL8 - one of the ship's tenders

CHAPTER 7

Offshore 3 - the other tender

A prescient advertisement for the Wonderful Isle of Man dating from 1957

View from the port deck

Roger Gale makes a point

Gone fishing!

Tom Lodge and Alan Turner

Two crew members relax

The relationship between Radio Caroline North and its host nation for almost four years were extremely cordial. But it didn't start that way. The djs on board *MV Caroline* were initially perturbed about the lack of response to the ship when they arrived in Ramsey Bay at 3pm on Monday July 6 1964. What they were ignorant of was that they'd arrived on the Isle of Man's National Day - Tynwald Day. Most Manx people were either in the centre of the Island at the Tynwald ceremony at St Johns, at home relaxing on the Bank Holiday or, if they were in the visiting trade, taking care of early season tourists. Added to this was the powerful concern that their local radio station Manx Radio, the tangible product of interminable negotiation with the Home Office and GPO, had only just made its faltering steps onto the FM dial.

While Caroline North boomed out across the Irish Sea at 199 metres on the popular Medium Waveband at a strength of 10 thousand watts Manx Radio, shoe-horned in a 30 foot caravan by the TT Course in Onchan, languished on the unpopular VHF (FM) band like Prometheus chained with a miniscule 50 watts barely covering the Isle of Man. It was a harsh stroke of fate which effectively ended its ambition to be a 'Radio Luxembourg of the Irish Sea'. Manx Radio's urbane managing director Richard Meyer (late of LM Radio) was characteristically generous to Caroline North but his chief executive John Grierson was witheringly critical of the GPO; the broadcasting regulatory arm of which had been unendingly obstructive to their operation but whose postal division facilitated a provision for Caroline North without batting an eyelid.

Caroline North's mountains of mail

THE WONDERFUL ISLE OF MAN

Radio Caroline North made no secret of its location and its affection for the Isle of Man. First impressions last and the fact that Caroline North arrived in July undoubtedly helped; the summer season was underway and the Isle of Man, with almost a hundred years experience of catering for mass tourism, knew how to help the patron to have a good time. The hotels and boarding houses were crammed with holidaymakers keen to make the most of the entertainment, scenery and friendship abundantly on offer. Also, unlike the Thames Estuary location where the coast was a narrow line in the distance the Isle of Man's spectacular landscape was very visible to the dj on-air. With Maughold Head looming in the studio window the djs, who received upwards of ten thousand fan letters a week, were never in any doubt where they were and they lost no opportunity in singing the praises of the charms and attractions of the 'Wonderful Isle of Man' to the audience. It was a powerful, subliminal image which penetrated the imagination of the millions of listeners located in the 300 mile sweep of its transmitter in Ramsey Bay. The singularly positive promotion of the Isle of Man to prime customers in the North of England, North Wales, Southern Scotland and Eastern Ireland wasn't lost on the Manx government. Tourism was then a major component of the Island's economy and the pragmatic nature of the Manx surfaced when, in September 1964, they placed advertising on the station.

Caroline North's Isle of Man liaison executive, George Hare, was based in the office in East Street, Ramsey. It was he who coordinated the operations on shore to complement the radio station on board. Christopher Moore was Programme Director in London but in reality hardly ever heard the station so it was left to the senior dj on board to interpret music policy and administer company policy. The djs worked two weeks on the ship, one week off and were paid for all three when they left the ship. They were entitled to one night's hotel accommodation and a flight from Ronaldsway to any direct destination when they departed on leave and on their return received two night's hotel plus a flight back. The ship's crew were accommodated at the Commercial Hotel, djs at the Mitre Hotel in Ramsey.

Dining in style

Tom and Jerry

Don Allen and crew relax

MV Caroline at twilight

Radio Caroline North on board *MV Caroline*

July 6 1964 - March 2 1968

Frequencies

- From 6 July 1964 1520 kHz - 197 metres
  (announced as 199 metres)
- From 19 December 1966 1169 kHz - 257 metres
  (announced as 259 metres)

Hours of Transmission

- To September 1967
  6am - 9pm (2am at weekend)
- After September 1967
  6am - 8pm (10pm on Saturday)

Equipment

- 2 x 10kw Continental Electronics 316 Transmitters
- 1 x Limiter to prevent over modulation
- 1 x Modulation monitor
- 2 x Daimler Benz generators

The broadcasting crucible of Caroline North

Studio

Installed by Ove Sjostrom and staff.
Technician operated until September 1964
Self-operated thereafter.

- 1 x Gates Studioette mixer
- 2 x Gates 16" turntables
- 2 x Gray Research tone arms
- 2 x Ampex tape recorders
- 2 x Spotmaster cartridge players
- 1 x AKG D12 microphone
- 1 x SG Brown headphones

News Booth

- 1 x AKG D12 microphone
- 1 x SG Brown headphones

Antenna

- 165' high heavily insulated, quarter wavelength folded dipole
- Sausage aerial forming the other leg
- Installation was by Arthur Carrington, Ove Sjostrom and the Greenore Port crane team.

Tom Lodge and canine friend

Weekend man
NICHOLAS HOLMES sails
out to the
floating jukebox

CAROLINE

The Che Sera

Jerry King

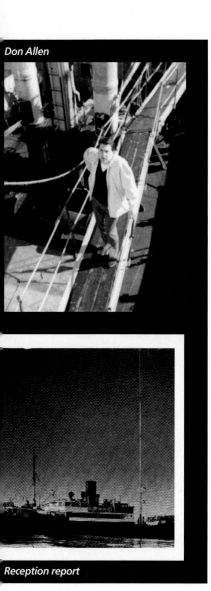

Don Allen

Reception report

MV Caroline's tender operated three or four times a week, often more. They brought changes of crew and djs plus fuel oil, fresh water, provisions (including eggs, cheese, pork, beef, chicken, milk, bread, vegetables and fruit), newspapers, radio spares, mail and approximately sixty records and thirty advertising tapes per week. Two boats were operated; *Essex Girl* owned by George Cowley, skippered by Harry Maddrell and *Offshore 3* owned by Offshore Tender & Supply Company based in Ramsey which additionally brought bonded stores from Holland. Radio Caroline North's shipping agent was the Ramsey Steamship Company who provided administration, telex and radio facilities with Offshore 3's owners. Because *MV Caroline* flew the Panamanian flag boarding her meant entering another country so HM Customs & Excise, Ramsey Harbour Board, HM Immigration, and the Police were involved in administering the tendering operations.

The *Che Sera* was a trip boat which made frequent excursions to Caroline North packed with sightseers. Several hundred tourists per season would make the journey to and around the ship although without

MARITIME MANIFEST

Customs clearance no one could board or alight either vessel; typically a visit from the *Che Sera* would bring djs and crew on deck, especially if the passengers included young females.

There were friendly relations with the Ramsey lifeboat; *Thomas Corbett* which was called out to the *MV Caroline* on four occasions in 1965 & 1966.

Addresses

To the ship - PO Box 3, Ramsey, Isle of Man

Advertising - 61 Lord Street, Liverpool 2
Tel: CENtral 8393

Head Office - 6 Chesterfield Gardens, London W1 Tel: HYDepark 9721

After August 1968
To the ship - Singel 160, Amsterdam
Administration - Grafton Street, Dublin

RADIO CAROLINE CLUB BALL
⊚ ZOWIE 1 ⊚

NEW BRIGHTON TOWER HALL
NEW BRIGHTON, NEAR LIVERPOOL

8th DECEMBER, 1965 ★ 7 - 11 P.M.

FREE - FREE - FREE TO CAROLINE CLUB MEMBERS

**YARD BIRDS ★ THE 4 PENNIES
BRIAN POOLE AND THE TREMELOES
THE HONEYCOMBS ★ TWINKLE
PAUL & BARRY RYAN** AND MANY ★ MORE ★ BIG NAMES
**GARRY FARR & THE T BONES
MARK LEEMAN FIVE ★ BILLIE DAVIS
RONNIE JONES** ★ **THE V.I.P'S
& THE BLUE JAYS** ★ **THE VAGABONDS**

Directed by Fred Perry

ALL CAROLINE CLUB MEMBERS WISHING TO TRAVEL WITH THE GROUPS PERFORMING
CATCH THE 12.20 P.M. TRAIN FROM EUSTON STATION, LONDON
Entertaining on the Train — The Rolling Kind

PROGRAMME SUBJECT TO ALTERATION WITHOUT PREVIOUS NOTICE

One of Caroline North's big events

THE PALACE BALLROOM

Dancing Nightly 8 p.m.

Bob Miller
and
The Millermen

Also featuring—

The Falcons : The Phantoms and The Ray Norman Combo

PLUS a Top Attraction Every Evening — including :—
THE WHO : THE KINKS : LULU AND THE LUVVERS : THE SMALL
FACES : BILLY FURY : THE HOLLIES : WAYNE FONTANA : THE
MINDBENDERS : THE FORTUNES : KENNY LYNCH : CRISPIAN
ST. PETERS : UNIT FOUR PLUS TWO : THE SPENCER DAVIS GROUP
DAVE BERRY : PAUL AND BARRY RYAN : CAROLINE D.J.s, etc.

Sunday Night Star Spectaculars including :—
CILLA BLACK and SOUNDS INCORPORATED : KENNETH McKELLAR
TOM JONES : THE BACHELORS : FRANK IFIELD : MAX BYGRAVES
ADELE LEIGH : DES O'CONNOR : DEREK DENE

Also EVERY WEEK—
ALL-STAR WRESTLING FREE-STYLE

Daily Surf Board Skating

SEE ADVERTS FOR FULL DETAILS OF PALACE ENTERTAINMENTS

THE PICTURE HOUSE
20th Century-Fox presents
RODGERS and HAMMERSTEIN'S
A ROBERT WISE Production
THE SOUND OF MUSIC
Produced in TODD-AO* AND COLOUR BY DE LUXE*
Starring JULIE ANDREWS · CHRISTOPHER PLUMMER
Produced by Argyle Enterprises Inc.

A typical Summer Season in Douglas

Don't forget

If you use a wireless set fitted in your motor car you must have a separate wireless licence

The use of a portable wireless set in your car is covered by the wireless licence for your home.

£1 for a motor car wireless licence at a Post Office

P.H.940
6/21(H.F.F.)

The GPO acknowledged the use of car radios was increasing

Caroline North's image fitted perfectly with the glittering summer line-up at the Palace Ballroom in Douglas

The replica ship was launched at the Palace Ballroom, Douglas in August 1965

Jimmy Savile

THE PALACE

Ray Teret and famous friends

SOLE SELLING AGENTS

PLANET PRODUCTIONS LIMITED · 6 CHESTERFIELD GARDENS · LONDON W.1 · HYDE PARK 9⁄.

INFORMATION

BIG BREAKTHROUGH IN COMMERCIAL RADIO SERVICES

CAROLINE AND LONDON DJs WITH BEATLES ON TOUR OF AMERICA

Radio Caroline and Radio London DJs will be accompanying
the Beatles on the complete tour leaving London on August
the 11th.

They will be two of the party of 12 actually travelling
and staying with the Beatles throughout America and the
only representatives of British Radio leaving London for
the whole tour.   .

Jerry Leighton's own personal up to the minute Beatle's
stories will be presented by Radio Caroline for their
listeners each day. Aged 29, Jerry was born in London
and educated in Canada. He was a Comedy Script Writer,
Fashion Designer, Actor, Comedian, Singer and Compere
before joining Caroline in June, 1964.

All Enquiries to:-

Frances Van Staden,
Press Officer,
6 Chesterfield Gardens,
London, W.1.

Telephone HYDe Park 9721
Evenings MAIda Vale 3140

55

Don Allen, Bob Stewart and Ray Teret

CHAPTER 8

VOICES FROM HEAVEN

Before the weekend of 4/5th July 1964 the radio listening public within a three hundred mile radius of the Isle of Man would have been tuned to Radio Éireann, the Light Programme, Home Service, Third Programme and Radio Luxembourg . Their listening habits would have evolved over years; they would have been more or less satisfied with what was offered. Radio wasn't something that people had strong views about one way or the other; it was just there.

Tom Lodge

VOICES FROM HEAVEN

Then Caroline North arrived off the Isle of Man to spark a radio revolution. The blend of Canadian, Australian and American professional announcers, plus a swelling group of home-grown willing amateurs, playing the latest pop music in an informal manner was a cultural shake-up on a grand scale. With hindsight it's easy to observe the path by which Radio Caroline North materialised but analysis with contemporary eyes (and ears) may obscure the genuinely enormous obstacles that were overcome to put the project together. Vast sums of money were risked. Cutting edge technology was used and raw announcing talent plunged into a situation which demanded knowledge and techniques which were acquired in swift succession.

It could have gone horribly wrong. The public could have simply turned on, listened for a couple of days and tuned back to their comfortable, respective state broadcaster or cross-border station dissatisfied with the programmes from a ship at sea. But it didn't; the people behind Caroline North had grasped the mood of the times.

They understood that the atmosphere was one of change and radio was an important part of it.

The listening public loved Caroline North's exuberant attitude, as elsewhere in popular culture rough edges were offset against appreciation of youthful enthusiasm. The regional accents, which appeared years before anywhere else, on Caroline North of Tony Prince and Ray Teret were a revelation. Before then the only regional accents from the North West on radio had been George Formby and Jimmy Clitheroe – and they never played the Beatles. The listening community sensed, perhaps unknowingly, that something was going on and they wanted to be a part of it. They wouldn't have articulated the notion that here were practitioners who'd had no opportunity to enter the world of radio, denied their chance of employment and development by the absence of a commercial radio industry but the audience was aware that there was a certain magnetism about Caroline North. Audience research indicated that up to sixteen million people were listening to the two Caroline ships, even after legislation the station was running neck and neck with the BBC's new pop channel with all its lavish resouces.

Caroline North was a public relations dream. The broadcast en route to the Isle of Man, Mick Luvzit and Jan Teret's wedding live on-air, the dj nicknames, the big prize competitions, the live appearances by the djs, the non-stop good humour and (relative) continuity of on-air staff all helped. Also helping was the geographic remoteness from head office in London. Free from day to day office tensions and with a virtual monopoly on the northern audience Caroline North's infectious team spirit, helped by the hothouse effect of being on-board non-stop for two weeks with no distractions, flowed to the audience. Tom Lodge, the first senior dj, played an important role in establishing the station's dj broadcasting ethos; 'enjoy yourself on air and the audience will enjoy it with you'. Tom's ego-free, enabling style meant that there was only ever a happy side to being on-air.

Caroline North's location was a vast benefit, not only in transmitter coverage terms. The sea helped with the radiation of the radio transmission but it also meant that a large collection of seaside resorts was directly in the transmission pathway. This meant that every summer season millions of men, women and children would head on holiday and day trips to the Fylde, North Wales, Southern Scotland, Eastern Ireland and the Wonderful Isle of Man. Unsurprisingly, Radio Caroline North would be playing on every holiday radio because pop music and seaside holidays went together. It's worth speculating that a large proportion of holidaymakers at Morecambe, New Brighton, Southport, Blackpool, Lytham St Annes, Cleveleys, Fleetwood, Llandudno, Rhyl, Colwyn Bay, Llanfairfechan, Grange-Over-Sands, Skerries, Mosney, Bangor, Portrush, Cardigan Bay, Ayr and the Solway, Dumfries and Galloway coast who'd never heard Caroline North previously would take the experience home and move their radio dial to the feel-good sound of their holiday. Irish Sea holidays had become an unseen marketing tool for audience building.

VOICES FROM HEAVEN

The voice of Caroline North fell silent in 1968. A poignant testament to the efforts and spirit of the characters who spoke into the microphone is that, forty years on, despite technical progress, changes of style and new ideas, this chapter of popular culture steadfastly retains its charisma.

"Daffy" Don Allen

Jim "Murph the Surf" Murphy

Mick Luvzit and Jan Teret congratulated by Captain Gips

VOICES FROM
HEAVEN

Daffy Don Allen

Jumbo Jimmy Gordon

Tom Lodge

Jason Wolfe
Fight For
Free
Radio

Rick Dane

Ric Jonns

Bob Stewart

Mick Luvzit

Mike Marriott

Jerry Leighton, Mike Ahern and Alan Turner

Tony Prince (centre) and Mick Luvzit

Yer Royal Ruler and Daffy

Daffy Don Allen

Mick and Don

Mike Marriott

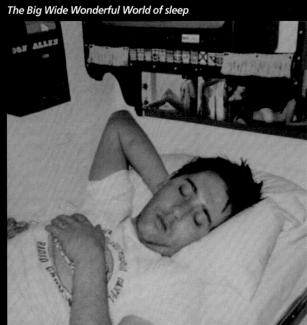
The Big Wide Wonderful World of sleep

Caroline news read by Nick Bailey

Jason Wolfe

VOICES FROM HEAVEN

Don and Bob put the world to rights!

Roger Gale

Jim Murphy

Mick Luvzit

Don Allen

Mike Ahern

Jerry Leighton

Mick Luvzit

Gordie Cruse

To Daffy Don
A Great Shipmate!
Gordie Cruse

Ronan O'Rahilly and Don Allen contemplate the future in August 1967

Nod Turner

Gordie Cruse

Ric Jonns, Tom Lodge and fans at Ramsey

Bob Stewart

Gordie Cruse, Kevin Duggan and Mick Luvzit at the re-opening of the Cavern

VOICES FROM HEAVEN: A TIMELINE

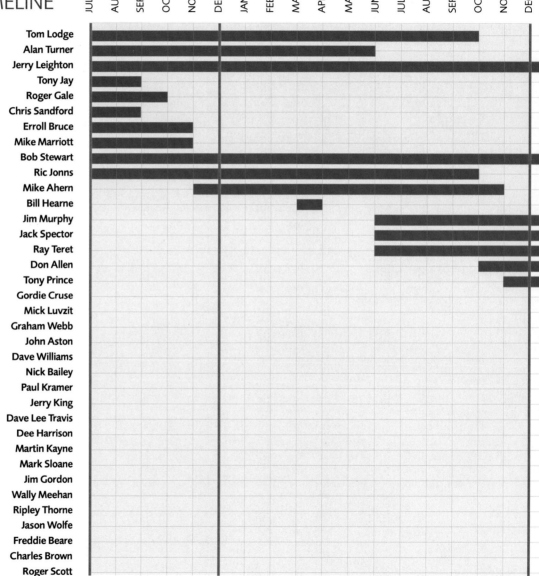

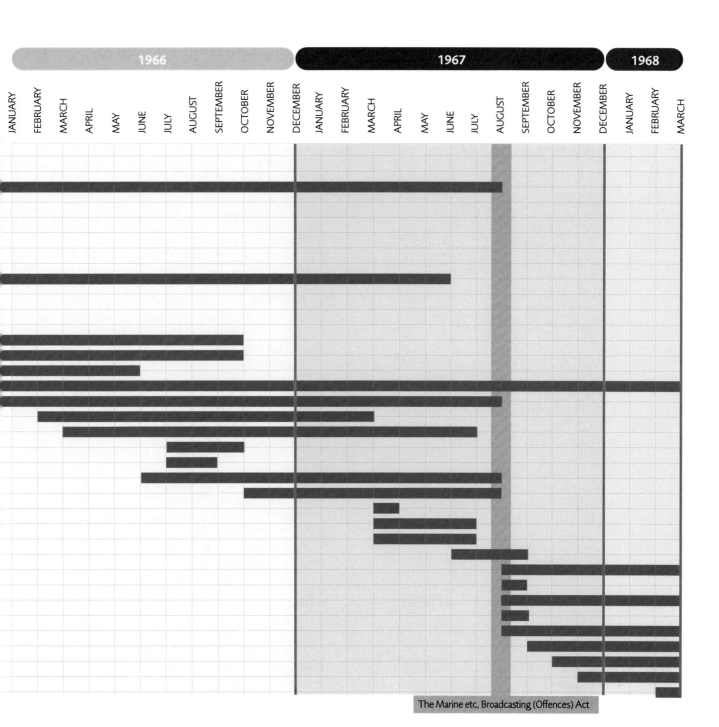

The Marine etc, Broadcasting (Offences) Act

Mark Sloane and Don Allen help "Harold Wilson" walk the plank at a Radio Caroline XI Football match at Onchan

CHAPTER 9

Radio Caroline North had always been a thorn in the UK government's side. Even before it came on-air, UK Postmaster General Reginald Bevins, had answered questions in the House of Commons concerning speculation about Caroline. He'd trotted out the familiar line that broadcasting commercial radio programmes from a ship would break international rules and agreements on the sharing of radio frequencies and would cause serious interference to radio communications in Britain and other countries. Legislation was hinted at.

Public reaction to the imposition of UK legislation on the Isle of Man

Ronan

DLT and a pensive Jerry King leave the ship on August 14 1967

Meanwhile the GPO officially requested ITU (International Telecommunications Union – the worldwide association which regulates broadcast frequencies and transmission powers) help to stop the pirate broadcasters. The ITU could do nothing but simply remind Panama of a provision in international radio regulations that the use of broadcasting stations on ships outside territorial waters was prohibited. In April 1964 the PMG told the Commons that leading advertising associations had given assurances that major advertisers would boycott the station, the record industry was collaborating and the GPO had cut the ship-to-shore radio link.

Without a hint of irony the GPO issued a warning that Caroline listeners were technically liable to prosecution under the Wireless Telegraphy Act of 1949 although it was conceded that it would be tricky to implement the law since no action could be taken against anyone who had tuned in by accident. During World War II no-one had been warned, let alone prosecuted, for listening to Lord Haw-Haw; it now seemed to some that Caroline was more of an enemy than Nazi Germany.

Mr. Bevins then met the Conservative Party's Radio and TV Committee; he spoke of his plans for pirate radio and local sound broadcasting in Britain. News leaked to the effect that he had postponed action against the pirates. In June 1964 Mr. Bevins committed the Tories to reviewing the subject of commercial broadcasting should they be returned at the October general election. Labour fervently condemned the 'greedy money-grabbing lobby agitating for commercial radio'. The Tories become associated with the land-based commercial radio lobby and Labour with preserving the BBC monopoly.

The politicians hadn't reckoned with the ingenuity of the offshore radio entrepreneurs. Though the Tories may have been embarrassed by the method of the venture and the socialists opposed in principle to the appropriation of what they saw as a national resource by commercial interests both were blinded by snobbery; offshore radio was perfectly above-board. The broadcasters broke no laws in force at the time. Their legal opinion devised a structure whereby the ship would be owned by a Panamanian concern and operated by a company in

TROUBLED WATERS

Liechtenstein which would then enter into contract with a UK company which sold the advertising time and paid a royalty to the ship owner. The seaborne staff would be paid from Liechtenstein through a subsidiary.

Radio Caroline North, and its ilk, ran full tilt into arrogance and political dogma. To the Labour Party, architects of nationalisation, free enterprise was an abomination; additionally they cherished the BBC as the sole, state-approved broadcaster. That anyone should have the temerity to challenge both of these assertions was an outrage. The Tories were by nature well-disposed to free enterprise but having introduced commercial television in 1955 seemed content to accept the 1962 Pilkington Committee's red light to commercial radio. They simply didn't see the point. Perhaps it's that both parties were colonised by individuals who were disdainful of popular culture, in particular the new working-class 'teenage' way of life that had emerged since the mid-1950s. The voting age would be 21 until 1970 so teenagers were not on the political radar except for the occasional criminal tendencies of 'juvenile delinquents'. Radio Luxembourg, by dint of history, was tolerated although given no official standing or facilities despite its large audience. The offshore stations, however, were a step too far for some politicians. The Tories would have preferred commercial radio on land, Labour wanted rid of them.

Labour squeezed past Alec Douglas-Home's Tories at the October 1964 election but with a majority of just four seats. Anthony Wedgwood Benn became Postmaster-General and wasted no time in announcing that new legislation would hit Caroline. However with such a slim Commons majority nothing concrete was planned for the time being. In January 1965 the Council of Europe agreed to prevent stations broadcasting from outside their national areas, conveniently forgetting Radio Luxembourg, Radio Monte Carlo, Europe 1 and others. Time seemed to be on the offshore stations side.

In March 1966 Labour sought a fresh mandate from the UK people and received an increased majority of ninety six seats and, although it was not in Labour's manifesto, offshore broadcasting was in their sights. What they couldn't do was make the radio stations illegal as they had no jurisdiction in international waters. However the advice they received indicated they could criminalise the supplying of goods and services to, working for and purchasing of advertising on the stations by British subjects and companies. This concept became the basis for the Marine etc., Broadcasting (Offences) Bill published on July 2 1966. Under the proposed law it would become unlawful to instigate, finance, provide goods or in any way aid an offshore radio station. The maximum penalty was to be two years imprisonment, a fine, or both.

By this time the cultural needs of the people had, at long last, oozed through to politicians who had conceded that the listeners to Radio Caroline North and its fellow broadcasters might not be content with the stodgy output of the BBC Light Programme, Home Service and Third Programme. They probably would have noted that by the date of the next election the voting age would be lowered to 18 allowing the enfranchisement of millions of youngsters who might remember who put their favourite pirate dj out of work. Something had to be done and the day after the Marine Offences Bill was paraded in the Commons the BBC announced that it had officially flagged to the Post Office 'the question of providing a continuous entertainment programme' to be carried on the Light Programme medium wavelength of 247 m. In March 1967 the UK Government moved the second reading of the Marine etc., Broadcasting (Offences) Bill. Soon after Postmaster General Ted Short announced Labour's answers to offshore radio; the Government planned more choice with a BBC popular music network by the end of 1967 and further choice in nine selected areas, as a preface to the creation of a network of BBC local radio stations. In July the UK's first local radio station, to be on-air in November, was named as Radio Leicester.

But the Labour politicians, Whitehall mandarins and BBC planners had neglected to remember that in the geographic centre of the British Isles memories were long. The Isle of Man had long revered the notion of a high-powered radio station based on the Island broadcasting to the UK, Ireland and beyond; Tynwald indicated its reluctance to ratify the MOA without a simultaneous increase in transmitter power for Manx Radio, the Island's own low-strength local station. Staunch opposition to such a compromise was met by a rejection of the Manx MOA by Tynwald's lower forum, the House of Keys. Upon the UK's indication that it would extend the directive via Order in Council the Keys resolved to petition the Queen, Lord of Mann not to sign the Order. The issue, described as "unique in Manx history" was that of the constitutional right of one state to make a law for another. The concern, on the Island, was that this was the thin end of the wedge which would see the UK assuming more control of the Isle of Man. Hitherto the UK had conceded that, in the majority of cases, the Island had the right to decide its own domestic laws but was adamant the subject of offshore broadcasting was an international one and thus it had entitlement to intervene. The ill-fated Manx delegation was stymied by the fact that the members of the Queen's Privy Council, who would present the petition from the Island, were the very people against whom they were remonstrating and unsurprisingly they refused to support the petition. A pungent row ensued; Tynwald was recalled from its summer recess by the Lieutenant Governor Sir Peter Stallard. After debate it was decided not to embarrass the UK government on the world stage (international media was packed into the public gallery) and to pursue the matter through the Commonwealth Secretariat. This policy was headed off by the UK Home Office which when, as the Isle of Man's international conduit, asked to present the petition accordingly simply didn't do so.

With new legislation looming times were grim for the offshore stations. The fort-based operations in the Thames Estuary had been closed down, prosecuted under the Wireless Telegraphy Act for being inside territorial waters. The remaining stations off the Essex, Yorkshire and Scottish coasts all indicated they would cease broadcasting to comply with the law. Only one station remained defiant; Ronan O'Rahilly was in no mood to let Caroline disappear, he painted a rosy future as an international radio station, managed from outside the UK but broadcasting to and anchored off its shores.

TROUBLED WATERS

The Marine Offences Act became law on August 15 1967 in the UK and, because the Queen was unavailable to sign the Order in Council in time, September 1 in the Isle of Man. The UK government's diplomatic and procedural strong arm tactics did not sit well with the Isle of Man's notion of its autonomy. The UK only has the right of intervention in the affairs of the Isle of Man in the event of the breakdown of civil order and on international matters - many saw this as paternalistic legislation; the dead hand of colonialism.

Don Allen

Labour peer Lord Stonham in bowler hat

It was ironic that whilst the GPO in the UK was trying to close Caroline North down, a GPO football team from St Helens played a Caroline XI at Onchan, Isle of Man in August 1967

The march to Government House

TROUBLED WATERS

The then Bishop of Sodor & Man claimed that emotion rather than reason had seized the Island and Canon John Duffield criticised Mec Vannin for organising a 500 strong march on Government House. He warned of mass hysteria - there was none and the Manx Constabulary's solitary police dog was not troubled. The march from the Rendezvous Cafe on Douglas Promenade to the Lieutenant Governor's residence was well-mannered and good humoured.

A crowd, including one hundred teenagers greets Lord Stonham on September 4 1967

The bacon & ham on the banner refers to Home Office Minister Alice **Bacon and** Lord Ston**ham**

Public protest

TROUBLED WATERS

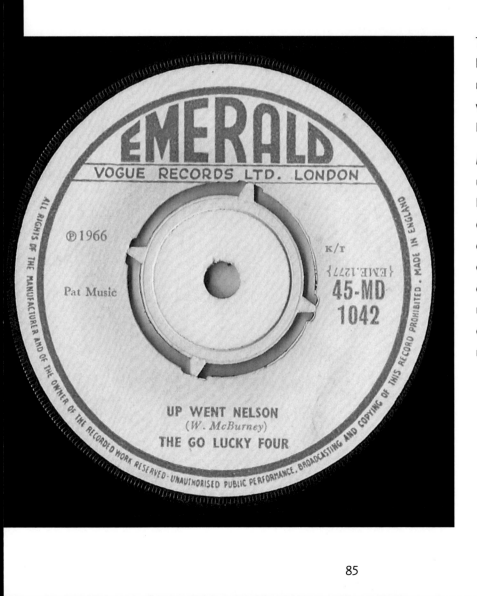

The appearance of the Go Lucky Four's smash hit 'Up Went Nelson' was misunderstood by many. It was the story of an incident in 1966 when former members of the IRA blew up Nelson's Pillar in O'Connell Street, Dublin.

Mervin Solomon's Emerald Records snapped up the recording and it was number one in Ireland for six weeks. Unsurprisingly, considering Caroline North's Irish connections, the song was featured heavily on air. Many interpreted this as an act of defiance against the British Government. In reality, the IRA at the time was a background organisation and in truth it was merely a manifestation of the Solomon connection.

MV Caroline under tow to Holland

On September 1 1967 with the Marine Offences Act entered in the Tynwald statute book Caroline North, as promised, continued broadcasting to her vast, loyal audience. Administration was from headquarters in Amsterdam via an office in Dublin and tendering, by the Offshore Tender & Supply Company of Amsterdam, from Dundalk, Co Louth. But advertising income had reduced to a trickle and revenues were only bolstered by payola – the charging of fees for playing certain records. This cut across the Caroline ethos (and harked back to the early 60s days of Radio Luxembourg) but was seen as a necessary compromise to maintain an on-air presence until times improved. Caroline North, albeit with new voices and slightly different music, still sounded lively and entertaining, the music still flowed and the audience remained immense. Behind the scenes though the story took another twist; the comparatively meagre funds accrued were not being utilised in paying a principal creditor.

On Tuesday February 27 1968 the tender *Offshore 3* arrived from Dundalk with supplies and a change of crew and djs. Four days later at midday on Saturday March 2

the Wijsmuller-owned tug *Utrecht* dropped anchor a mile away from *MV Caroline* in Ramsey Bay. This was nothing out of the ordinary as vessels often sheltered at this location for various purposes however it's worth speculating that the new members of the crew would have recognised her as a member of their employer's fleet. The station closed down at 10pm that evening after Don Allen's 'Country and Western Jamboree' had been broadcast. Shortly after 2am a loud thump was heard as the *Utrecht* came alongside Radio Caroline North, members of her crew boarded the ship and, in a well planned operation, removed the transmitting crystal and sealed the studios. The captain was informed that the ship was to be towed to Amsterdam by order of the Wijsmuller Group, owners of the Offshore Tender & Supply Company, as security until Caroline's liabilities of over £30,000, increased by the recent devaluation of sterling, were settled. Unknown to the staff on *MV Caroline* an identical scenario was being played out off the coast of Essex on board Caroline South's *MV Mi Amigo*.

TROUBLED WATERS

Sunday March 3 dawned and millions of Caroline North listeners tuned in vain to 259 metres for their favourite station unaware of the drama now being played out off the Isle of Man. The *Utrecht's* crew went about their task in a businesslike but not unfriendly manner, the anchor chain was cut, and a line was attached between the two vessels. Later that day on Monday March 4 at 6pm the mute, barnacle encrusted *MV Caroline* was hauled from Ramsey Bay and, almost 44 months after she arrived in a boisterous intensity; the Radio Caroline North era was over.

MV Caroline arrived in Amsterdam on March 9 and remained there, with writs nailed to her mast, unguarded and prey to looters and squatters. On May 29 1972 her fate was sealed when Frank Rijsdijk-Holland of Hendrick Ido-Ambacht paid 26,500 guilders for her forty two year old metal, she was scrapped by Van de Marel of Ouwerkerk in Zeeland.

Dutch tug Utrecht with Caroline North in tow

DAILY SKETCH. Monday. March 4, 1968

SILENT CAROLINE TOWED AWAY

The victors. Leeds players hold cup aloft.

RADIO CAROLINE, the last defiant pirate radio station, may have gone off the air for ever.

That was one theory put forward last night to explain why the station's two ships were being towed to unknown destinations after staying silent all day.

Both Caroline North and Caroline South went off the air on Saturday night.

Soon afterwards a Dutch tug began towing the South ship away from her base off Frinton, Essex.

And Caroline North, based off the Isle of Man, was taken in tow by another Dutch tug the 638-ton Utrecht.

Last night the Utrecht's captain, Martines Meeldag, said: "I don't know where I'm due to sail for. I expect further instructions once I am under way.

SHAUN USHER and PHILIP JORDAN

until someone tells us what is going on."

Both stations have been having generator problems and disc-jockeys have warned listeners that there might be "a fairly short close-down for maintenance."

Bedside vigil

Caroline
THE RADIO PIRATE
towed off the air

By TERRY PATTINSON

THE reign of Radio Caroline, queen of Britain's "pop pirates," came to an undignified end last night when the ship was towed away into the Irish Sea by a Dutch tug.

The rusty, barnacle-encrusted Caroline, first and last of the floating pirates, went into "exile"—probably for ever.

fight for FREE RADIO

join us...send s.a.e for free associate membership

FREE RADIO ASSOCIATION
239 Eastwood road Rayleigh Essex

The abandoned, looted studio

TROUBLED WATERS

Caroline North and Caroline South impounded in Holland

A sad end for Caroline North - awaiting the breakers blow torch in Ouwerkerk, Zeeland

Sister ships together in Amsterdam for the first time since March 1964 in Greenore

CHAPTER 10

LEGACY

Radio Caroline North, along with her sister ship, left a lasting inheritance to subsequent generations of broadcasting practitioners and fans: additionally she left Manx and UK political legacies.

On September 30 1967 the BBC Light Programme separated to become Radios 1 & 2. Radio 1 was a direct response to the wave of enthusiasm created by the offshore pop stations of which Caroline was the first. The style was unashamedly based on the pirates' format with mostly ex-pirate djs and the same jingles. Radio 2 continued the Light Programme mixture of cheerful announcers, soap operas (Mrs. Dales Diary, Waggoner's Walk) and light popular music programmes for many years.

LEGACY

An eight station BBC Local Radio experiment started on November 8 1967 with Radio Leicester taking to the air with a mixture of spoken features, phone-ins, news, music programmes, live music and political debate. Originally co-funded with local authorities it was deemed a success and continues to date with forty stations gaining varying degrees of audience penetration.

UK commercial radio arrived with the Heath government after the unexpected Conservative victory in the June 1970 General Election. The Tories introduced the Sound Broadcasting Act 1972 which gave the newly-created Independent Broadcasting Authority responsibility for appointing contractors for nineteen 'independent' (the phrase 'commercial radio' was steadfastly avoided) contractors in specific areas. On 8th October 1973 LBC (London Broadcasting Company) became the first legal commercial radio station to broadcast to and from the UK, followed by the other eighteen stations over the next three years. The Labour government of 1974-1979 unsurprisingly halted the proliferation but when Margaret Thatcher entered Downing Street the commercial radio industry expanded exponentially. There are now three national commercial stations and over three hundred local, regional and community stations.

In Ireland legal commercial radio arrived in 1989 after many years of successful land-based pirate radio. Currently two national, four regional and twenty five local stations operate under the aegis of the Broadcasting Commission of Ireland (BCI). Radio Telefis Éireann (RTÉ) offers populist programming via Radio 1 and 2fm in addition to three other channels.

Manx Radio was purchased from its private owners by the Manx government in 1968. It is held in trust for the Manx people and funded by a mixture of subvention and advertising revenue. Its low power was increased to cover the Isle of Man; it celebrated 40 years on the air in 2004 and still broadcasts a highly popular eclectic mix of programmes. It now faces competition from two Isle of Man based commercial stations, the owner of one - Energy FM - is politician Juan Turner, the son of David 'Nod' Turner of Caroline North.

Manx politics was profoundly affected by the Radio Caroline North episode. The constitutional crisis brought into sharp focus the prevailing attitude in Westminster which contrasted with the notions of greater independence sought by certain Manx politicians and sections of the public. In particular the experience of the 1967 Marine Offences Act sharpened the Isle of Man's resolve regarding Britain's proposed entry into Europe. Manx politicians succeeded in negotiating a Special Treatment Protocol whereby the Island is not a member of the EC but continues to trade freely. On another level the Isle of Man continued to have aspirations to host a high-powered radio station. In 1999, freed from UK interference it awarded a license to broadcast on 279AM (Long Wave) at 500 kilowatts to Isle of Man International Broadcasting. The station would have easily covered the UK North and Midlands plus, Scotland, Ulster and Eire but the project never materialised. One wonders what Ronan O'Rahilly would have done with the opportunity.

Radio Caroline North ended in 1968 but the Caroline story continued off the south coast. Although the *MV Caroline* was broken up in Holland the smaller Caroline ship, *MV Mi Amigo*, survived and surreptitiously left harbour in 1972 to re-commence transmissions off the Dutch coast. She continued throughout the 70s until she sank in a storm in March 1980. Radio Caroline returned with a new ship *MV Ross Revenge* in 1983 but a combination of government legislation and storms forced her off-air in 1990. Since then Caroline has broadcast on satellite and the internet.

The generation of fans who listened to Radio Caroline North is now in its fifties and above. It's a fitting tribute to the impact that this short-lived radio station had that, forty years on, the mere mention of the radio station, the music it played and the personalities who played the records will ignite memories, conversation and smiles. In addition new students of the station find themselves captivated by its audacity, élan and accomplishments - Radio Caroline North lives on. I do hope you enjoyed this book and the Manx National Heritage exhibition 'Pirates Of The Irish Sea'.

LEGACY

Chris Sandford with the Caroline North Roadshow

Bob Stewart

CHAPTER 11

CAST OF CHARACTERS

Don Adlerslight bading a Cambrian Airways Viscount at Ronaldsway

CAST OF
CHARACTERS

Mike Ahern was born on September 30 1942 in Crosby, Liverpool. He worked in a clothing boutique, as a barman, clerk and in the Cavern Club. He wrote to Radio Caroline with typical ebullience informing them that they really should be employing the best dj in England - Michael Ahern! He was invited for audition and soon got the call to Ramsey. His infectious wit and irrepressible charisma proved an immediate success, 'Your dj Mike A' hosted the 9-Noon slot and became the housewives' favourite. In 1965 both he and Tom Lodge were transferred to Caroline South to implement a new programme format and boost floundering audience levels. With an eye to the future Mike left Caroline in the spring of 1967 to get his foot in the door at the new BBC Radio One. It worked, but not for long. He was featured in the famous photo of the original Radio 1 team but, on 8th October 1967, Mike Ahern co-hosted his one and only Radio One programme, the second edition of Top Gear. Mike headed for Australia and for the rest of the 60s and throughout the 70s weaved his magic on 4BC, 6PM, 3UZ, 2KO and 7HT. In 1988 Mike retraced his steps and featured on Capital Gold, Essex Radio, Radio Aire, Piccadilly Radio, Country 1035 and North Norfolk Radio. He lives in Norfolk.

Don Allen was born Donald Jorge on March 8 1939 in Winnipeg, Manitoba of Russian/native Canadian parentage. He attended broadcasting school in Chicago and returned to north Manitoba for his first position then worked at CFAR, CHTM and CKPR across Canada plus, stations in the USA and Mexico. He married an English girl, and came to London to meet his in-laws. On the brink of returning to Canada with his wife Sandy he heard about Caroline and quickly made himself known. His services were snapped up by Caroline but a bad bout of sea-sickness on the South ship confined him to shore-based duties at Caroline House. Vacancies on the North ship in 1965 led to a temporary stay in Ramsey Bay where Don found the larger *MV Caroline* far more stable and comfortable than the *MV Mi Amigo*. He remained with Caroline North until the end in March 1968 and his was the last voice ever heard on the station. His programmes The Big Wide Wonderful World of Daffy Don Allen and Country and Western Jamboree were central to Caroline North's essence and his confident good humour imbued the station for three years. Don was Senior dj until Caroline's closure when he returned from domicile in Ireland to Onchan, Isle of Man with his wife, son and daughter. In 1970 he joined Manx Radio, worked in nightclubs on the Island and also presented a country music show on BBC Radio Merseyside until 1977. In September 1972 he returned to sea as Programme Director with Radio Nordsee International until 31 August 1974. After a spell out of radio he returned to Ireland in 1981 and featured on Sunshine Radio, Radio Carousel in Navan, ERI in Cork, CCR Cavan, Ernside Radio, Radio West Mullingar, Radio Star in Monaghan, Nova in Dublin and finally Tullamore's Radio 3 in the Midlands. On 13th May 1995, following a heart attack, Don Allen died.

John Aston was born in March 1943 in Maidenhead. A man on many radio names he was born John Hatt, in 1965 he became John Stewart on KING Radio housed on a disused ack-ack fort in the Thames Estuary. When KING was replaced by the more powerful and successful Radio 390 he changed his name to Chris Stewart as an Equity registered actor had the rights to the name. He remained Chris Stewart in November 1965 on the other side of the Thames on the disused Knock John naval fort that housed Radio Essex. In May 1966 he joined Caroline North as a newsreader but as there was a Stewart (Bob) already on-air he became John Aston. He left Caroline North later that year and after selling advertising for Radio England and a stint on Caroline South he joined Radio 270 off the Yorkshire coast. In April 1967 he transferred to the short-lived Radio 355. John then entered the film industry garnering an impressive career as a special effects technician on dozens of films including Titanic, Goldeneye, Krull, Alien and The Fifth Element. His love of radio still shines as he broadcasts regularly on Blast 1386 at Thames Valley University in Reading.

Nick Bailey was born in London 1947. As the son of actor Robin Bailey he seemed destined for a life on the boards, he joined a theatre company in Plymouth and worked in the publicity department of London's Mermaid Theatre. In September 1966 his first break in radio came when he joined Radio Caroline South as a newsreader shortly afterwards heading to Caroline North in November 1966. He remained off Ramsey until August 1967 and the introduction of the Marine Offences Act. In 1968 he emigrated to Australia on a £10 assisted passage ticket then moved to Hong Kong where he presented classical music programmes. He then joined British Forces Broadcasting Service with postings to Gibraltar, Cologne, Berlin and Hong Kong rejoining Radio Hong Kong in 1985 presenting daily current affairs. He became the Hong Kong correspondent of the newly created BBC Radio 5 in August 1990 and when offered a position in 1992 at Classic FM, the UK's first national commercial station, Nick came home. His was the first voice on Classic FM and he remains there to date, personable, popular and highly experienced.

Freddie Beare was a team member of the Caroline South broadcasters which challenged the Marine Offences Act and continued after August 14 1967. Born as Ross Brown in Queensland, Australia, he worked in radio in the late 50s at 2SM Sydney, 2BS Bathurst, 7HT Hobart, Tasmania and 2XL Cooma, New South Wales. He headed for Britain in 1965 to join Radio City on a fort in the Thames Estuary working as 'RWB', Radio 390 on shore then just before the MOA became law he joined Radio Caroline South as Ross Brown. His stay on the MV Mi Amigo was short, he decided Caroline North sounded like a great adventure changed his name to 'Frantic Freddie Beare' and stayed with the station until the enforced closure in March 1968. He was on board the Caroline North ship when it was towed away and remained in Amsterdam to wait for instructions which never came. Returning to London for an abortive attempt at record promotion in London Freddie Beare plus compatriot Jim Gordon returned to Amsterdam to work in discotheques first at the King's Club then the Hilton Hotel. He married his Dutch girl friend Patricia and returned to Australia. He worked for 2LM Lismore and 2KM Kempsey in New South Wales then in 1971 decided to go back to school and on to University. He joined the Australian Public Service then the Australian Foreign Service in 1975. He served diplomatic postings to Jakarta, Malta and the Netherlands returning to Canberra in January 1991.

Charles Brown was born Terry John in Western Australia on March 8 1945. He appeared on the *MV Caroline* after the passing of the Marine Offences Act legislation although his arrival on board was given an inordinate build-up. 'Lord' Charles Brown, as he was sometimes known, joined Caroline North in November 1967 amid mock ceremony. Also known as Charlie Brown he presented the 6 - 8pm show and read the news bulletins throughout the day. He stayed with Caroline until the station closedown in March 1968 and now lives near Johannesburg where he occasionally broadcasts on Swazi Music Radio.

Erroll Bruce was born in Alexandria, Egypt, in October 1942. He was brought up in Canada and joined Radio Caroline in April 1964. He appeared on Caroline North and South and left in 1966 to join Radio England. In 1967 he returned to Canada and worked on the CBC, CKFH, CHUM-FM and Q107. Now resident in Toronto Erroll's long-established UFO radio programme *Strange Days...Indeed* also appears on the Virtually Strange Network website.

Roy Carr is an eminent rock music journalist whose first career was as a musician. He become a staff journalist at New Musical Express in the 60s and later edited NME, VOX and Melody Maker magazines. He was an 'inner circle' journalist who was a close friend to many rock legends including John Lennon and Phil Spector and wrote influential biographies on The Beatles, David Bowie, Elvis Presley and The Rolling Stones. His father, Tony Carr, is famous for writing 'March of the Mods' (Finnjenka Dance) for the Joe Loss Orchestra. Roy's connection with Radio Caroline North stems from his artistic ability; in 1965 he designed the famous dj t-shirts for Jim Murphy, Don Allen, Tony Prince and Jerry Leighton; at that time he was working in above-the-line advertising for Coca-Cola and Polaroid. He also designed the 'Bring Back Caroline' t-shirt (copying the BBC logo) for the demonstration in Trafalgar Square.

Jennifer Conway is the name behind the sultry female voice frequently heard on announcements in 1964. She never visited the ship but recorded her broadcasts in London where she was appearing in the West End.

Allan Crawford was a man who loved turning ideas into action. He was a music publisher in the 1950s who later owned his own record labels, a talent agency and management office. He soon learned the power of the BBC when it came to non-established publishers and record companies. When he heard about the Scandinavian offshore stations, he was hooked. In 1962 he attempted to buy the Swedish offshore station Radio Nord and broadcast to Britain. The

ship now renamed the *MV Mi Amigo* was set to broadcast but his backers feared government interference and the ship was sent back to the Texas coast. He eventually raised the finance for the ship and it sailed back to the UK in late December 1963. Crawford had approached many people during 1963 to attract backing and music including entrepreneur Ronan O'Rahilly who saw the potential straightaway but instead of joining Crawford's Project Atlanta, Ronan planned his own station - Caroline. Both ships were fitted out at Greenore, O'Rahilly's father's port and inevitably Radio Caroline was the first to leave and broadcast, Crawford's Atlanta was a distant second. The two stations were side-by-side and advertisers were loath to buy airtime. An uncomfortable coalition was formed in July 1964 with Crawford's Atlanta remaining off East Anglia as Radio Caroline South and O'Rahilly's Caroline sailed for the Isle of Man to become Caroline North where it enjoyed a northern monopoly. Within six months Crawford's Caroline South faced overwhelming competition from Radio London and entered a year of low morale and a slump in advertising revenue. By the end of 1965 Caroline South was almost broke and Crawford was bought out by O'Rahilly. He stayed on selling airtime and quietly observing the emergent authority of Phil Solomon who, having purchased a shareholding, eventually outmanoeuvred O'Rahilly. Returning to the music business, Crawford put his experience to good use by producing the most successful series of cover version albums albums ever; the Pickwick label's 'Top of the Pops' LPs. He became involved with Scientology in the 70s and even studied to be a high priest. What money he had was enthusiastically committed to the religion. By the mid-80s Allan had lost both legs and eyesight to diabetes. He spent his last few years in a nursing home in Anglesey where he died in December 1999.

Jimmy Duggan, along with his brother, was in charge of the Liverpool office of Caroline North at 61 Lord Street. He returned to Ireland after the demise in 1968.

Kevin Duggan was the promotions director of Caroline North at the Liverpool office at 61 Lord Street. Little is known of his subsequent career.

Gordie Cruse born in Calgary, Alberta in 1942 climbed aboard Caroline South as a newsreader in August 1966 before swelling the Canadian contingent on the Caroline North ship where he continued to read the news but also presented programmes. Gordie stayed on the *MV Caroline* until March 1967 when he embarked on travels to Rome, Athens, Cairo, Kuwait, New Delhi, Hong Kong and Hawaii before returning to the microphone in 1968 at CFQC Radio in Saskatoon. After more travel, to Australia, he took up the post of Operations & Music Director at CFAX 1070 in Victoria BC in 1969. In 1976 he left radio embarking on a career as a supervisor in the Youth Justice Services division of the Ministry of Children and Family Development. He retired after 26 years unbroken service and lives on Vancouver Island. He is the author of *Juvie: Inside Canada's Youth Jails* a book examining Canada's juvenile penal system.

Rick Dane was heard as the host of Lucky Birthday Bonanza on Caroline North. The competition was pre-recorded at the Caroline House studios in Chesterfield Gardens W1 and played out simultaneously on both ships. Born Randall Gautier in Mauritius in 1941 he appeared on Springbok Radio in South Africa in his teens and compèred touring pop concerts. After arriving in England he became resident dj at the Wimbledon Palais ballroom and studied acting at the Webber Douglas Academy, performing in a stage version of The Knack and acting alongside Vanessa Redgrave in The World's Baby at London's Royal Court Theatre and appearing in the film The Mini Affair with Georgie Fame, Clement Freud, Clive Dunn, Roy Kinnear and Willie Rushton. His radio career began in the Thames Estuary on the Radio City fort in 1965; he joined Caroline the following year and stayed until mid 1967. He was contracted to co-host Top Gear on Radio One at its launch but did not stay long. Throughout the 70s Rick worked in club promotion in the UK, Europe and the US. He is now based in Miami providing audio-visual facilities in the hospitality industry.

Jerry Duncan was the man behind the 'Sound Of A Nation' jingle package. He was heard occasionally as an announcer on Radio Caroline during the early days of the station but was mainly employed behind the scenes as a producer, making taped programmes on land and recording commercials. Born in 1937 in London, he served in the RAF before finding work as assistant to film director Lewis Gilbert. He worked on Light Up The Sky and Sink The Bismark before moving into television in 1960 as a cameraman with ATV. He joined Caroline in 1964 and stayed until January 1967. He died during the seventies.

Roger Gale was born on August 20 1943 and is the only Caroline North dj to make it to the UK House of Commons. A descendant of Sir Francis Drake he was born in Poole, Dorset. After studying acting at the Guildhall School of Drama he joined Radio Caroline North in August 1964 and left in January 1965. He joined the south ship in June 1965; Caroline South was suffering from the competition of Radio London's Top 40 format and part of the attempt to update Caroline South's middle-of-the-road sound was to term djs 'Good Guys', a presentation theme pioneered by WMCA New York and transferred to 2SM Sydney. It wasn't successful and another change in programme policy followed when Tom Lodge and Mike Ahern journeyed south from Ramsey. The upheavals saw Roger move to join Radio Scotland as Programme Director and then launch Radio 270 off Scarborough. After the Marine Offences Act became law Roger joined BBC Radio London as a reporter then producer of Today on Radio Four and Newsbeat on Radio One. He switched to television, working on Thames TV's 'Magpie' then entered politics. Always active in politics having been a member of the Tory Party since 1964 he was elected Conservative MP for North Thanet on 9 June 1983 (defeating Cherie Blair) and remains there to date.

Martin Gips was the Captain of *MV Caroline* for most of 1966 and 1967. Born in Rotterdam in 1946, he was a relaxed individual who spent a lot of his time reading legal text books intending to train as a lawyer. Unlike other captains he readily came to terms with a posting on a ship that remained at anchor at sea. It was he who officiated (in a borrowed uniform) at the wedding of Mick Luvzit and Jan Teret.

Bill Glendenning was a radio engineer on Caroline North.

Jim Gordon was first heard on Radio 390 under his real name Guy Blackmore where he remained until it was closed down by the UK government. Australian by birth, he was not precluded from working by the Marine Offences Act so changed his name to 'Jumbo Jim Gordon' and joined Radio Caroline North. After the *MV Caroline* was towed away he formed a record plugging company with his Caroline colleague and fellow countryman Freddie Beare which although successful was not financially viable. He became a continuity announcer on BBC TV, Southern TV and Thames TV. After a spell in South Africa in the 70s he returned to Australia and was heard on 5AD and 5AA in Adelaide. Jim Gordon died of cancer in 2004.

Trevor Grantham was a radio engineer on Caroline North.

George Hare was Caroline North's Liaison Officer based at 3 East Street, Ramsey. Born in Dublin in 1936 he was a childhood friend of Ronan O'Rahilly. This brought George to the position of responsibility for all aspects of the Caroline North operation in the summer of 1964. George's smooth, meticulous manner ensured that personnel, supplies, wages and relations with officialdom were handled with efficiency and charm. After Tynwald reluctantly accepted the Marine Offences Act George operated the Caroline office in Grafton Street, Dublin and coordinated the Dundalk tendering operation. After the demise of the station he went into the TV aerial business then became an insurance broker. Now retired he lives in London.

Dee Harrison from New Brighton on the Wirral was 21 when he joined Caroline North just before the Marine Offences Act came into force on mainland Britain. He served during the 'phoney war' interregnum until the UK legislation was forced on the Isle of Man and stayed until October 1967. His offshore career blossomed again in 1972 when he joined as Mark Slate Radio Nordsee International off Scheveningen, Holland. He returned to Merseyside to work at Vauxhall Motors in Ellesmere Port under his real name of Derek Powell.

Roy Hastings appeared on Radio Caroline North almost every day it was on the air yet never set foot on board.

His was the voice on the C-A-R-O-L-I-N-E jingle which was edited from his 1963 Decca single Caroline, a tribute not to the radio station (which in any case it preceded) but to the wife of his boss. London born Roy Hastings was the resident compere at the Garrick Club in Leigh, Lancashire which was one of two clubs owned by Roy Jackson, the other being the Caroline Club (named after his wife) at nearby Atherton. The Garrick Club, opened in November 1961, was a forerunner of the cabaret clubs which abounded in Britain through the sixties and seventies when huge stars, including Leigh's own Georgie Fame, would appear on a weekly basis supported by a resident band plus compere and comedian. When the Garrick Club was closed to make way for a bakery in 1978 Jackson had already sold it and retired - first to St Annes then to the Isle of Man and after seventeen years at the Garrick Club Roy Hastings returned to his roots in the south of England.

Bill Hearne was the voice of the hugely successful Caroline Cash Casino competition which was responsible for over a million postal entries in three months. Born in London on 6th August 1927 he moved with his parents to Toronto at the age of three. He went back to London aged 17 to attend college returning to Canada to become a commercial artist additionally studying broadcasting and working in radio. In 1964 he returned to the UK and, after a spell with Radio Luxembourg, joined Caroline North in April 1965. Bill was Programme Director for the South ship until January 1966 transferring to Radio London in June of that year. He only stayed three months before returning to Caroline. It was during his second spell with Caroline that he became the host of Cash Casino, with its ground-breaking cash prizes, broadcast hourly every morning on both Caroline ships. With its multi-million advertising sales ITV's top quiz programmes Double Your Money and Take Your Pick could still only offer the very distant promise of £1000, BBC TV's quizzes occasionally awarded a paltry £50 in Premium Bonds. Caroline Cash Casino routinely paid out thousands of pounds and Caroline House became stuffed to overflowing with sacks of entries. After six months four million entries, all with a sponsor's proof of purchase enclosed, had been received. After his time with Caroline Bill returned to Radio Luxembourg then disappeared from view until he worked as a technical model-maker for the Open University TV programmes.

Abraham Hengefeld was born in 1917 was the captain in charge of the *MV Caroline* on the renowned journey which brought her to Ramsey Bay. Her destination was unknown until, live on-air, he opened the sealed orders and proclaimed in a thick Dutch accent that the destination of the radio ship was the Isle of Man. He left the ship a few weeks after anchorage in Ramsey Bay to deliver a trawler to Mexico, replaced by Captain Baeker the skipper who had originally taken the ship from Greenore to East Anglia.

Tony Jay born in Glanamman in 1939 and subsequently educated at the London School of Economics. He became a teacher in Essex and was also a part-time ballroom dj. He met Jimmy Savile who suggested a career on Caroline. Tony joined Caroline North a week after she arrived off the Isle of Man and left in the autumn.

Ric Jonns was born on January 26 1943 in Thorpe, Norfolk. Richard Turton was a ten-pin bowling instructor in Oldham in the early sixties when he met Tony Prince, then a club dj. He helped Richard, now christened Ric Jonns, become a dj at the Oldham Astoria. Ric also took lighting responsibilities at the Manchester Plaza where he met a local lad called Peter Noone from the beat group Herman and the Hermits. Their career was starting to take off and Ric became their road manager. While they became Herman's Hermits and headed for stardom Ric joined Radio Caroline in late 1964 first on the south ship then to Ramsey Bay. He left after a year to work, at Peter Noone's suggestion, in America. He was well known at WAIR, Winston-Salem, North Carolina but returned to the UK after three years to be involved in band management and, prematurely, skateboarding. He returned to the US in the late seventies to teach soccer. Whilst living there, he was tragically killed in a car accident in 1985 at the age of 42.

Martin Kayne was born October 27 1943 at Gravesend, Kent. Whilst posted to Cyprus serving in the RAF catering corps he worked at the local forces radio station. His broadcasting appetite thus whetted he bought himself out of the RAF and applied to the offshore fort-based Radio Essex which he joined in January 1966 as Michael Cane. He moved to the short-lived Radio 355 and became Martin Kayne. When Radio 355 was forced off the air by the UK government's introduction of the Marine Offences Act Martin looked for a position. Because of the sudden vacancies on the *MV Caroline* after some of the existing Caroline North djs left rather than break the law, Martin joined Caroline North in August 1967 and stayed until the ship was towed away in March 1968. His broadcasting career was revived briefly with Radio Nordsee International in 1971 but subsequently his catering career took precedence. He wrote a page in Short Wave Magazine for many years under his real name of Andy Cadier. He occasionally broadcasts on community stations in Kent.

Frank Kemble was a studio engineer on Radio Caroline North in 1964

Jerry King was born in Welland, Ontario on May 2 1941. His beefy build (6' 2") led him to a career as a PE teacher but radio intervened and he appeared on Welland Radio plus CKLB-AM and CKQS-FM in Ontario and for ZBM radio and television in Bermuda before heading for the UK to experience the Swinging 60s. He joined Caroline South in March 1967 and transferred to the North ship in April where he stayed until the introduction of the Marine Offences Act at the end of August. He then headed back to London did some acting in commercials and joined United Press International as a reporter. After a brief stint with UPI in New York he returned to London in 1971 where he became the London radio freelance news operative for the US network ABC. Gradually he was asked to do more TV reporting around the world before signing his first TV contract in 1975. He worked in most European countries, East and West, in a dozen Middle Eastern countries, and Southeast Asia. It must have seemed to US viewers of World News Tonight With Peter Jennings, Nightline, 20/20 and , Good Morning America and other network news programmes that wherever there was a war Jerry King would be in front of a camera. He covered the conflicts in Northern Ireland, Lebanon, and Vietnam, he reported on the fall of Communism in Poland, Czechoslovakia, East Germany and Hungary and interviewed hundreds of international politicians including Yasir Arafat, King Hussein of Jordan, Lech Walesa, the Shah of Iran and Ayatollah Khomeini. After heart surgery in 1993 he moved to Washington DC to cover the US State and Defence Departments and then the White House. Jerry retired in 1997 and currently lives in Ontario. He enjoys life and travels extensively.

Henrik (Hank) Koning is Frisian by birth and Manx by residence. Born in May 1939 he was already a time-served merchant seaman by trade when offered a position with the Wijsmuller company on the Offshore fleet of tenders servicing the East Anglian floating radio stations. He was attached to Caroline North tendering operation and was involved until March 1968. He married a local Manx girl and returned to Groningen but the call of the Manx hills was too strong, he has lived in Ramsey for many years where, in retirement, he breeds Texel sheep and restores vintage agricultural machinery.

Paul Kramer was born in North London in 1947. He was a film industry sound engineer who joined Radio City in 1966. "Your dj PK" moved to Caroline North in March 1967, leaving a month later to join Radio 270 off the Yorkshire coast. Paul was sadly killed in a car accident on Putney Bridge in December 1968.

book Success Without Goals, set up the International Breatherapy Association, managed his son's pop group and worked with a Californian project called Radio One Earth. After, in 1995 he moved back to the UK but returned to America having been a disciple of Zen in India and the US for many years. Tom is now known as Umi. His disciples have created an ashram around him in Santa Cruz, California where he gives Satsang to those searching for inner peace.

Jerry Leighton was the daily breakfast host on Caroline North for the first three years of its life. His infectious sense of humour, original comedy material, slick presentation and engaging manner entertained millions and inspired a generation of youngsters; Jerry 'Soopa' Leighton even had his own theme tune Super-Duper Man by Jimmy Cross. He, Don Allen and Bob Stewart defined the sound of the station but as illegality drew near he dropped from public view suddenly and permanently. Born in London in 1936 he was brought up in Canada and returned to the UK at the age of 19. He worked as a fashion designer, compère, singer, comedian and script writer before joining the original Radio Caroline off the Essex coast in 1964. When Caroline merged with the rival Radio Atlanta, Jerry stayed on the *MV Caroline* broadcasting throughout the journey to Ramsey Bay along with Tom Lodge and Alan Turner. Although 'Soopa' Leighton presented The Leighton Early Show on Caroline North for over three years he temporarily left the ship 1965 to work in Caroline HQ in London and in 1966 was chosen to report for Radio Caroline on The Beatles tour of the USA sending back daily bulletins from within the tour party. When the Marine Offences Act loomed Jerry left Caroline North in August 1967 and has never broadcast since. He operated an antiques business in Hampshire with his wife and now lives in retirement

Tom Lodge was destined to work in broadcasting. His grandfather, Sir Oliver Lodge, was one of the pioneers of wireless telegraphy. Tom was born in Forest Green, Surrey, in 1936 but his family moved to America during World War II. He went to school in the UK but returned to Canada on his eighteenth birthday. He worked as a cowboy, spent two years on an expedition into the frozen wastes of the Canadian Arctic, and then joined CBC, the Canadian state broadcaster, gaining a posting to London. There he met Ronan O'Rahilly in a pub and Tom found himself joining Radio Caroline off the Essex coast just after its first broadcast. When the ship sailed to the Isle of Man to become Radio Caroline North Tom, Jerry Leighton and Alan Turner broadcast all the way. Tom stayed on Caroline North through most of 1965 but transferred to the South ship when floundering ratings and new competition meant a new sound was called for. Tom was aboard the south ship, *MV Mi Amigo*, in January 1966 when she lost her anchor and was washed up on the beach. He presented the Breakfast Show on both ships and was senior dj/ Programme Controller but later that year after disagreements over music and salary Tom left, working briefly for the BBC before returning to radio in Canada. He became Head of Communications at the University of Ontario, farmed jojoba nuts in Costa Rica, wrote a second

Mick Luvzit is the dj who got married live on Caroline North. Born William Brown on February 24 1944 in Portage La Prairie, Mantitoba. He was a talented musician and singer who also worked in radio at CKY, CHWO, CHIC, CHUM and CFGM before heading for the UK. He initially joined Caroline South in June 1966 before moving to the North ship. He was a big success and received over a thousand fan letters in his first week on air. He also released a record on Decca called 'Long Time Between Lovers'. Whilst on Caroline North he met Janet Teret the sister of a fellow Caroline dj 'Ugli' Ray. They began dating and there was talk of marriage. Mick suggested that they should capitalise on the romantic idea of being married at sea by a ship's captain and tie the knot on board. The wedding took place on 20th September 1966, performed by the Caroline

Captain Martin Gips and with a commentary on Caroline North from news-chief Graham Webb. They had one daughter and although divorced during the seventies they both live in British Columbia. Mick is still active in radio, broadcasting in Vancouver.

Don Lydon was the Caroline North airtime sales representative in Ireland.

Harry Maddrell was the skipper of PL8 Essex Girl, which along with *Offshore 3*, visited the *MV Caroline* bringing food, supplies, radio spares and personnel. *Essex Girl* was owned by local businessman George Cowley.

Mike Marriott was born in Leicester in 1941 he attended an English grammar school then continued his education at Dartmouth College in New Hampshire. He gained a degree in drama in the States but lack of success led him to become a radio disc-jockey on WTSL in Lebanon, New Hampshire until his return to the UK in 1964 when he joined Radio Caroline North. Mike stayed just a few months with Caroline returning to the US and Canada to work in theatre and television. Never one to stand still Mike appeared as an entertainer on board cruise ships, joined a back-to-the-land hippie movement, got involved in the Native Indian protest movements and qualified as a Fireground Commander in the Fire and Rescue Service. More recently he has spent time

involved in peace building processes in international conflict zones leading initiatives to establish community reconciliation projects between former enemies. Mike has been active in Africa, South Asia and the Middle East. He now lives in northern Italy.

Bob Marshall-Read was a radio engineer who worked on Caroline North from August 1966 until April 1967.

Wally Meehan had been a guitarist and vocalist with the Nevada Showband in Ireland, he joined Caroline North just before the introduction of the Marine Offences Act and left a few weeks later. Whilst in London on business he'd met Ronan O'Rahilly who remembered him from the showband days and offered him a dj position. He left the station as the UK legislation was about to be enforced and accompanied Ronan on the flight back to London. Wally returned to the live music business then worked in the in-store radio industry for twenty years before moving to Spain where he broadcasts on TKO Gold FM on the Costa Blanca.

Christopher Moore was the Radio Caroline's first Programme Director. He was born into an Irish-American family in Washington DC in 1941 and came to the UK at an early age. He later served in the Merchant Navy and worked in advertising before going into the music business. His friendship with Ronan O'Rahilly led him to be heavily involved in the launch of Radio Caroline off East Anglia. It was Chris who facilitated the introduction to one of the main financial backers, Chris coordinated the purchase of the *MV Fredericia* which became the *MV Caroline* and it was Chris who presented the very first show on British offshore radio on Easter Saturday 1964 dedicating the first record - The Rolling Stones' Not Fade Away - to Ronan. He didn't remain at sea for long but came ashore to work as Caroline's first Programme Director at the office in Chesterfield Gardens. He stayed until 1967 and subsequently worked as a successful freelance photographer.

Jim Murphy was born in Beeville, Texas on March 24 1940 (Easter Sunday) and grew up in Tuleta between San Antonio and Corpus Christi. Fittingly for his eccentric persona his boyhood hobby was the 1930s craze of 'pole squatting', he once spent 49 days up a pole! He appeared on many Texas radio stations, including KAML, WAKY, KILT and KIBL before travelling to Europe in 1965. Big Jim (6'5") was en route to Spain but paused in England and never got any further east. After a brief stint on Radio Caroline South, he moved to the North ship and it was there that he made his name as Murph The Surf with his Midnight Surf Party and Country & Western Jamboree. Jim returned to the States in 1966 and served in the military in Vietnam, afterwards he continued to work in broadcasting. He retired on health grounds in 1990 but was incapacitated due to a long standing condition contracted while serving in Asia. He lived out the remainder of his days in Austin, Texas, Murph the Surf died in June 2000.

Martin Newton was a radio engineer on Caroline North.

Ronan O'Rahilly was born in 1939 into a wealthy, well-connected family in Clundalkin just outside Dublin. He moved to London in 1961, operated nightclubs and managed pop musicians and singers. His musical ambitions were thwarted by lack of radio play so when the opportunity to run his own radio station presented itself he took it with both hands. He was at the helm of Radio Caroline and Radio Caroline North from their beginnings until his position was undermined by new investment in 1965. After closedown in 1968 he continued to be the charismatic figurehead of the Caroline movement, retaining his enigmatic status despite Caroline's diminishing rank. He continues to live in London with no hint of a biography in sight.

Phil Perkins was a radio engineer on Caroline North.

Tony Prince was the only offshore disc-jockey to have been a real jockey before although only for a short time. Born Thomas Whitehead in Oldham, Lancashire on May 9 1944 he went on to be an apprentice toolmaker and member of Manchester group The Jasons. He became a Top Rank ballroom dj in Bristol and presented an early ITV pop programme, Discs-A-GoGo for Television West & Wales. On one of the shows Radio Caroline's Tony Blackburn made an appearance to plug his latest record Tony asked him for contact details, organised an audition and joined Caroline North in December 1965. He transferred to Caroline South briefly then returned to Caroline North and 'Your Royal Ruler' became one of the station's most popular presenters. He stayed until the introduction of the Marine Offences Act in August 1967. Tony Prince went on to Radio Luxembourg rising to the position of Programme Director and since then he has been heard on Capital Gold in London and XTRA-AM in Birmingham. In the late 70s he spotted the potential of club culture and started the highly successful Disco-Mix Club and the spin-off magazine Mixmag. He currently runs the satellite TV channel Wedding TV.

Christopher Sandford was the only member of Coronation Street ever to be a dj on Caroline North. Chris was born in London in 1939 and, during 1963, had played Walter Potts in Granada TV's Coronation Street. Walter was a milkman who became a pop singer and the song featured in the programme, 'Not Too Little Not Too Much', became a Top 20 hit for Chris which resulted in an appearance on Thank Your Lucky Stars. He released a number of other singles including 'You're Gonna Be My Girl' with backing band The Coronets, featuring future Jimi Hendrix Experience drummer Mitch Mitchell. During 1964 Chris worked in the sales department in Caroline House, the station's headquarters, but he also hosted promotional events and briefly broadcast on Caroline North for a period of about six weeks in 1964. After leaving Radio Caroline Chris continued to make records, including a Bob Dylan spoof called 'I Wish They Wouldn't Always Say I Sound Like The Guy From The USA Blues'. He also had a Top 30 hit in Spring 1975 as part of a duet with the gravel-throated voice-over star Bill Mitchell. They appeared under the name 'Yin and Yan' in a spoof of Telly Savalas' hit version of 'If'. Chris continued to act and appeared in films such as Half A Sixpence, Deep End and Up The Chastity Belt plus TV's The Persuaders, Dad's Army and notably in a 1966 episode of ITV's Danger Man entitled Not So Jolly Roger about a pirate station based on a Thames estuary fort where his character, a dj, is murdered and pushed into the sea. Chris now lives in Sussex.

Roger Scott was born in north London and joined the fort-based Radio Essex in 1966 despite having no previous radio experience. He moved on to Radio 270 off Yorkshire, then Radio 390 before climbing aboard the *MV Caroline* on the final tender trip from Dundalk just five days before the ship was towed away in March 1968. He returned to sea and joined Radio Nordsee International as Arnold Layne in April 1972. After RNI his stentorian tones were heard on numerous radio and television stations, principally in East Anglia, under his real name Greg Bance. Nowadays he lives in Kent where he writes poetry.

Ove Sjostrom was Chief Radio Engineer on *MV Caroline* from her inception 1964 until February 1965. He arrived at the project with considerable experience as prior to Caroline North he'd been chief engineer on Radio Nord off Stockholm. After leaving Caroline North, he continued to build studios and work for both state and private radio in Sweden. He now lives in Torsås, where he is an active radio ham.

Mark Sloane began his offshore radio career as Mark Hammerton on KING Radio, one of the Thames Estuary fort stations which later became Radio 390. Born 7th March 1942 in Somerset Mark was one of Radio 390's best known voices and, after a year, he was approached to join Radio Caroline South where he became Mark Sloane. After a short period on Radio Antilles, Montserrat, he returned to the UK and joined Radio 355 where he stayed until it closed down in August 1967 just ahead of the Marine Offences Act. Radio Caroline was determined to carry on despite this new law and needed djs so Mark returned to Caroline and this time joined the North ship. He stayed until late 1967 when an article in a newspaper identified him personally, he felt it wiser to leave the station than risk prosecution under the new law. His professional radio career ended there but a highly successful livelihood in the advertising industry has occupied him since

Philip Solomon is an old-fashioned, larger than life, show business character. Born in Belfast in 1926 where the family business, Solomon & Peres, was record distribution and retail. His father Louis had become a shareholder in Decca during the 1950s giving the family influence in Decca through Dick Rowe, the man who was to turn the Beatles away. Additionally Philip's brother Mervin owned Emerald Records in Ireland. In the early sixties Philip moved his operational base to London and concentrated on artist management. He was involved with such diverse talents as Van Morrison, Ruby Murray, Bridie Gallagher, Phil Coulter, Raymond Lefevre, The Dubliners and The Bachelors. He started his own record label Major Minor Records whose releases and artists received heavy airplay on Caroline North. Solomon admitted that he wouldn't have invested in the station if he hadn't had control over the music played. Viewed from today's perspective this may appear unethical but at the time wasn't blinked at; Radio Luxembourg had blatantly rented its airtime to plug records for years, Radio London had its own publishing house and Reg Calvert, the pop-manager owner of Radio City, bought the station from one of his own artists (Screaming Lord Sutch) and played his own talent stable constantly. After Radio Caroline, Phil's artist management career continued, he secured an agreement with Hughie Green whereby he would represent the winners of Opportunity Knocks which led to him guiding the careers of Pam Ayres, Frank Carson and Lena Zavaroni among others. He later opened Solomon Art Galleries and became a force in the art world. He lives in Belfast with his wife Dorothy.

Manfred Sommers was Chief Radio Engineer on Caroline North from 1965 until closedown. Austrian-born, like Caroline's overall chief engineer Paul Dale, Manfred was extremely popular on-board and seemingly took very little leave. He accidentally provided many funny voices for Don Allen; his German accent struggling to cope with Don's scripts was a feature of The Big Wide Wonderful World of Daffy Don Allen.

Jack Spector was Caroline North's slice of authentic New York. His show was the only American Top 40 radio heard on British radio in the 1960s. Every weekday evening from May 1965 to October 1966 Jack would play the best of the Billboard Hot 100 shriek, roar, bellow, ring bells, throw in sound effects and hammer home his catch-phrases "Your Main Man, Jake", "Your Leader", "Your Boss With All The Hot Sauce". He encouraged his subjects to take the pledge; "Raise Your Right Hand And Repeat After Me - I Will Have No Other Leader After My Leader, Jake." His sign-off was identical - "Look Out Street, Here

I Come". The programme, sponsored by Roulette Records, built up a loyal following and was a genuine addition to Caroline North's Beat credentials. Jack Spector was born in Brooklyn on September 17th 1928, attended Brooklyn College and had a minor league baseball tryout for the Brooklyn Dodgers. After serving as a US Army sergeant in Korea he fixed his eye on a radio career first in 1955 in Martinsburg, West Virginia then Albany NY, Providence Rhode Island and Chicago. His big break came in 1961 when he became one of the original WMCA Good Guys of New York City he became a radio giant. He had authentic pop connections too; the Four Seasons hit 'Sherry' was named after his daughter Cheri. Jack Spector continued broadcasting in America for many years after his Caroline North audience last heard him. After WMCA he was found on WCBS-FM, WHN, WNBC, WPIX and WQCD but on 8th March 1994 after a 33 year continuous presence on the air in metropolitan New York Jack Spector suffered a heart attack live on-air at WHLI in Garden City, Long Island. He died later that day at Winthrop University Hospital.

Bob Stewart was born Graham Stewart on July 3 1939 in Liverpool. Bob did national service in the army in Aden then worked in various local clubs after becoming a dj at the suggestion of Pete Best, the original Beatles drummer. He joined

Radio Caroline in 1965, spending one month on the South ship before transferring to the North. He was advised that his Liverpool accent might alienate listeners so he developed the very authentic sounding mid-Atlantic accent we now know and love. 'Baby Bob' presented the noon-3pm show. "Your Bobby baby who loves you so crazy" stayed with Caroline North until July 1967. After a fallow period he joined fellow Caroline North dj Tony Prince at Radio Luxembourg and stayed for eighteen years. In 1987 he moved to Dallas, Texas for a time but returned to Europe and was heard again on Luxembourg as well as Jazz FM, Red Rose Radio, Capital Gold and others. He also appeared on BBC 1 TV in Jim Davidson's Big Break as 'Frank the Yank'. In 2002 he moved to Dallas where he currently lives.

Sheridon Street was a radio engineer on Caroline North. Sheridon Keith Street (born 1941 in Blackburn, Lancashire) was a keen Caroline North listener and, as a qualified electronic engineer, wrote to the Chesterfield Gardens office asking for a job. After interview he was given £70 expenses and told to report to MV Caroline immediately. After two tours of duty off the Isle of Man he was transferred to Caroline South where he stayed until early 1967. Now retired, he lives in Thailand.

Ray Teret was born in Salisbury, Wiltshire. He worked as a warehouse clerk, apprentice heating engineer and waiter at the Mecca Ritz Ballroom in Manchester before landing his job with Radio Caroline. Ray owned up to be being somewhat economical with the truth at his Caroline audition; "I said I'd worked in a Mecca dance hall for two years. I didn't lie to them. They never asked me if I'd played records!" He joined Radio Caroline North in August 1965 and became known as 'Ugli' Ray Teret. Ray opened a boutique on North Quay in Douglas, Isle of Man which was run by his sister Janet, through her brother Janet got to know the other Caroline djs. She met and fell in love with Mick Luvzit and married him live on-air on 20th September 1966. Ray had left the station in August 1966, his subsequent career has encompassed spells on Piccadilly Radio in Manchester and Signal Radio in Stoke-on-Trent.

Carl Thomson was a visiting radio engineer on Caroline North. He was based on the original Radio Caroline but transferred to the South ship. He left the Caroline Organisation in May 1967.

Ripley Thorne served one short spell on board *MV Caroline* in September 1968.

Dave Lee Travis joined the Caroline Organisation in September 1965 at the age of 20. He was on the South ship for two years before transferring north. He was born David Griffin on May 25 1945 in Buxton, Derbyshire becoming a designer after finishing his education. He also became Dave Lee Travis spinning records at the Oasis Club in Manchester and through the club scene he became acquainted with Herman's Hermits who offered him the position of tour manager. A former member of the Hermits' entourage and fellow Manchester dj Ric Jonns had gone to join Radio Caroline and Dave followed his trail. DLT joined Caroline South in 1965, where he took on lunchtime duties, and stayed until June 1967 before heading to the north ship, he stayed until the legislation in August. Dave had a continental TV career during his stint on Caroline; he presented Beat Club on NDR in Germany. After Caroline he waited patiently for a position at the BBC securing weekend work then the daily breakfast show which he presented as 'The Hairy Cornflake' plus BBC World Service's Jolly Good Show. In 1976 he had a hit record with former Manx Radio dj Paul Burnett under the alias 'Laurie Lingo & The Dipsticks'. He famously resigned live on-air from Radio 1 in 1994 and has presented syndicated shows on commercial radio plus BBC local radio.

Alan Turner was one of the three broadcasters who performed the ultimate long distance show – from Harwich to Ramsey. Alan was born in Blackheath, London, on March 29 1939. Living in Singapore he first entered showbiz aged 19 as well as spending time as a salesman, engineer and policeman before becoming a disc-jockey. Known as 'Neddy' after the character in The Goon Show, he joined Radio Caroline in 1964 initially as a technical operator. In the early days of Caroline the announcers had technical operators to play the records for them and Alan took on that role before moving to the other side of the microphone. He left the ship, ran a successful retail/wholesale business with his wife Elaine and then turned to aviation. For many years they have operated an aviation maintenance facility in Kent. Ironically one of their aviation projects is the operation and maintenance of the aircraft used by Invicta Radio for their 'Flying Eye' road traffic reports. So although no longer broadcasting he is actively connected with commercial radio.

David 'Nod' Turner was a 19 year old apprentice carpenter at Ramsey Shipyard when he made big news in 1964 becoming the first Manxman to work for Caroline North. He happened to be at the bar in the Commercial Hotel on Ramsey quayside when a foreign sounding man asked if anyone knew anything about tape recorders and sound engineering. As the bass player in a beat group Nod had produced the band's recordings and felt qualified to assert his claim, within a couple of minutes Caroline North radio Chief Engineer Ove Sjostrom had hired him as a technical operator on the *MV Caroline*. He remained with the station until 1966 when he became road manager and part-time bass player with The Rockin' Vickers, a Blackpool based group who had great regional success plus a strong following in Europe. He later returned to the Isle of Man where he operated retail and electronic communications businesses. His son, politician Juan Turner, owns Energy FM, a commercial radio station on the Island.

Graham Webb was news director for the Caroline network organising the Newsbeat bulletins for both ships. He was born in Parramatta, New South Wales on 19th April 1936 and entered radio via Rod Taylor, the film star, who asked Graham's help in playing a practical joke on a colleague. Rod suggested Graham take up acting

but Graham moved up the ladder in Australian radio and decided to try Europe. He stopped off at Radio Monte Carlo, Radio Norway and the Voice of Germany before joining Radio Caroline South in May 1965. Initially a dj he became responsible for the news team and notably the commentary on offshore radio's only on-air wedding, that of Mick Luvzit to Janet Teret. He was also heard again on British radio in the 70s presenting the Australian segment of World Wide Family Favourites on BBC Radio Two. He also became a familiar face on Australian TV as host of the Australian version of Blind Date. Graham currently operates a radio station on the Sunshine Coast in Queensland, Australia.

Eddie White had firm maritime connections, his grandfather was a top Aberdeen trawl skipper and his father had served in the Merchant Navy during World War II. He was born in Aberdeen and worked in the print room of a local weekly newspaper before becoming a promotions man working on land for Radio Caroline before becoming a dj on the Caroline North ship. He left to join Radio Scotland where he stayed until the Marine Offences Act closed it down. He died in Blackheath, London in 1990 in his early fifties.

Dave Williams was born in Oswestry, Shropshire. He spent nine years as a photographer in the RAF and spent off-duty time working for forces radio. He had decided on a career in radio on leaving the Air Force. Initially frustrated by negative responses from the BBC, Radio Luxembourg and BFBS Dave met Graham Webb who was formulating Radio Caroline's Newsbeat service. In May 1966, still in the Air Force, David spent three weeks as David Wynne on the Caroline South ship. He was offered the task of launching the news service on Caroline North. He left the RAF and stayed with Caroline North, working as a newsman and occasional dj, until the Marine Offences Act in 1967. On leaving Caroline he joined Border Television then, after more TV announcing on both commercial and BBC, Dave returned to radio at BBC Radio Leeds. In 1972 he moved as a producer on Pebble Mill at One on BBC 1. Additionally he also produced a number of light entertainment specials for the BBC with Don McLean, Neil Sedaka, Peggy Lee, Anne Murray and the Three Degrees. He stayed at Pebble Mill in Birmingham until 1983 when he left to establish a new career in IT in Belgium.

Jason Wolfe was announced as a 25 year old South African when he appeared on the post-Marine Offences Act *MV Caroline* in August 1967. Such was the apprehension over the extent to which the UK government would go to enforce the law – imprisonment was a real threat – that Chris Bowskill from Cheshire became Jason Wolfe. Following his time with Caroline he worked with Jim Gordon organising live entertainment in London pubs. He was also one of the people behind the land-based pirate Radio Free London and it was also reported that he was working as a croupier. In June 1974 he briefly returned to sea when he joined former colleague Don Allen on Radio Nordsee International off the coast of Holland. He also wrote magazine articles for Wavelength and Script promoting commercial radio. He and his wife moved to San Francisco in 1976 where he worked with the PBS public service network and KALX, the Berkeley University radio station. They returned to the UK in 1983 plus son Drummond and daughter Polly. Jason worked in local radio in London and lectured on media liaison. Additionally he was a jobbing actor in films and TV. His health started to falter and in 1986 he died of cancer.

Mike Wright was a radio engineer on board the *MV Caroline* from October 1966 until March 1968. An electronics engineer by trade he left Pye Ireland after hearing about a vacancy on Caroline North. Upon joining he immediately felt at home on the ship which he found happy and comfortable. He was responsible for maintenance of the studio and transmitters and remembers that Chief Engineer Paul Dale made sure that there was a healthy budget for equipment and spares ensuring that Caroline North was very rarely off-air and that the studio functioned efficiently. As an Irish citizen he wasn't affected by the UK Marine Offences Act so stayed with the station until the end. Mike wasn't on-board when she was towed away having left to go on leave five days earlier. After Caroline he went into the sound equipment hire business in Dublin, in the 70s he joined RTE as a studio engineer where he remains.

TOGETHER AGAIN IN THE 90'S...

After being together on and off the coast of the Isle of Man, Bob, Tony, Mike and Paul were back together again at Capital Gold in 1996.

Photographs included herein have come from many sources. It has proved unfeasible to trace the owners of all images. If copyright has been infringed the publishers will endeavour to rectify in the next edition.

Acknowledgments

The author gratefully acknowledges the help, forbearance and encouragement of;

Stephen Harrison, Kirsty Neate, Matthew Richardson, Roger Sims and all at Manx National Heritage.

Quintin Gill MHK

Mike Ellis, Roger Watterson and all at The Copy Shop.

Patch Allott, Greg Bance, Nick Bailey, Norah Barnes, Alan Bennett-Turner, Penny Bowskill, Dec Cluskey, Terry Cringle, Gordie Cruse, Scott Fybush, Frank Gallagher, George Hare, John Hatt, Ben Healy, Len Hulme, Martin Kayne, Jerry King, Hank Koning, Hans Knot, Ingemar Lindqvist, Mick Luvzit, Mike Marriott, Svenn Martinsen, Peter Moore, Christine Moughtin, Jon Myer, Chris & Mary Payne, Mike Plumley, Paul Rowley,

George Saunders, Ian Sinclair, Philip Solomon, Brian Stowell, Sheridon Street, Carl Thomson, Kenny Tosh, Chris Turner, Nod Turner, Umi, Martin van der Ven, Dave Wilson, Mike Wright, Gerry Zierler and many others.

If you would like to comment on this book or have information or reminiscences you wish to pass on please e-mail chesterfieldpublications@manx.net

The 40th Anniversary Caroline North Convention takes place over the weekend of 20/21 September 2008. Many former Caroline North djs, executives and personalities will join fans and students for a weekend of memories of and tributes to a wonderful radio station. For details of how to purchase a delegate place e-mail: carolinenorth@manx.net

26/4/09 (G)